Chris C. Pinney, DVM

Guide to
Home Pet Grooming

Everything about your Pet's Skin and Coat, Including Nutrition, Basic and Advanced Grooming, and the Latest Information on Parasites, Allergies, and Other Common Skin and Hair Coat Disorders

Photographs by Dennis Dunleavy, Jill Mathis and others
Illustrations by Sandra G. Pinson

BARRON'S

All inquiries should be addressed to:
Barron's Educational Series, Inc.
250 Wireless Boulevard
Hauppauge, NY 11788

International Standard Book No. 0-8120-4298-0

Library of Congress Catalog Card No. 90-34722

Library of Congress Cataloging-in-Publication Data

Pinney, Chris C.
    Guide to home pet grooming / Chris C. Pinney.
      p. cm.
    ISBN 0-8120-4298-0
        1. Dogs—Grooming. 2. Cats—Grooming.
      3. Dogs—Diseases. 4. Cats—Diseases.
      5. Veterinary dermatology. I. Title.
      SF427.5.P56   1990   90-34722
      636.7′0833—dc20   CIP

PRINTED IN HONG KONG
56   9927   98

Foreword

Congratulations! You've just taken the first step toward a healthier pet. Using the *Guide to Home Pet Grooming*, you'll learn the easy and correct way to care for your dog or cat's skin and hair coat. You'll also learn about common skin diseases and disorders, and how to recognize and manage them before they get out of control.

As applied to dogs and cats, *grooming* is a much misunderstood term. Grooming involves more than the weekly trip Bo Bo makes to the local doggie beauty salon, or the decision about which color nail polish Fifi should wear with her red satin sweater. Grooming is not only a way to cosmetically "beautify" dogs and cats and maintain breed standards, but also a significant part of your pet's preventive health care. Did you know that, by far, the majority of pet health problems seen by veterinarians involve in one way or another the skin or hair coat? Many of these problems could have been avoided if the owners had recognized the need for routine grooming—not at the local grooming shop, but in the pet's home environment. Pet owners can use grooming techniques to help maintain and improve their pets' overall health. It is no accident that beautiful coats and supple skin seem to come naturally to healthy animals!

The *Guide to Home Pet Grooming* concentrates on those grooming fundamentals that pet owners can apply in their own homes, including brushing; bathing; ancillary care of the eyes, ears, nails, and teeth; nutrition; and external parasite control. A section is included that covers dermatopathies, or disorders of the skin and hair, complete with photos and the latest scientific information. Also included are sections on professional grooming techniques for dogs and cats (for those wishing to learn how to keep their pet's coat looking good between trips to the grooming salon) and on first aid for grooming injuries.

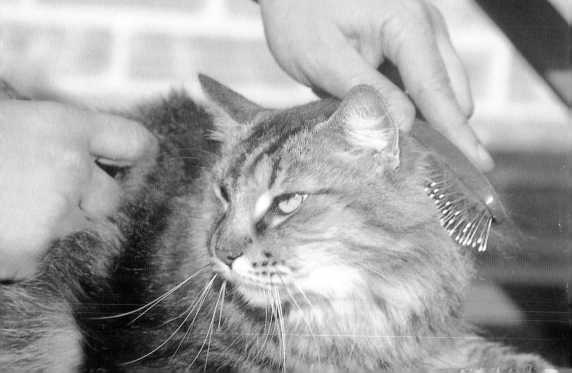

Contents

Chapter 1

A Question of Grooming

Many misconceptions exist regarding home pet grooming. Let's dispel a few here and now by answering the three most common questions asked by pet owners regarding this subject.

Question 1: *Animals in the wild never get groomed by people. Why do I need to groom my pet?*

The key word here is "wild." Mother Nature takes care of her own very well in the wild. For example, shedding cycles, which are based on the natural change of seasons, occur in a timely manner in the wild. Natural terrains not only help wear down the nails, but also remove and comb out dead hair from the coat as animals move through thick underbrush and trees. Unlimited exercise and a diet as nature intended certainly contribute to healthy skin and hair coat. And, very importantly, the anatomic features of wild animals, such as hair coat length, tend to be naturally adapted to geographic location and climate.

If you apply the above examples to the average house pet, the reasons for routine grooming should become crystal clear. The artificial lighting found in the home and elsewhere often disrupts or changes the natural shedding cycle of a pet. In comparison with natural terrains, carpets and grass are hardly as effective at wearing down toenails or removing dead hair. When it comes to a pet's diet and exercise, table scraps and poorly formulated pet foods often take the place of a well-balanced diet, and the daily exercise program may be a mere ten-minute walk around the block. And finally, dogs and cats are often poorly adapted to the climate and environ-

Grooming allows you and your pet to spend that all-important time together.

ment they're kept in. This can lead to increased stress, skin allergies, and other related health problems.

It is not my intent to imply that every wild animal is the picture of perfect health and immaculate grooming, while our poor pets suffer from neglect and hair mats. But I think you get the point. Pet dogs and cats cannot and should not be compared to their wilder counterparts. They must be treated and cared for differently.

Aside from the fact that pets whose skin and coats are kept in top-notch condition by routine grooming look good and feel good, there are two other reasons to groom. First, though you may not realize it, your pet savors every second spent with you. That affection may not be as obvious as you would like it to be, but it exists nonetheless. By grooming on a regular basis, you will help fulfill this basic need of your special friend. Second, while working on your pet you can be on the lookout for any abnormalities that may signify an underlying disease process. Many diseases of pets, such as infections, parasites, diabetes, and cancer, can manifest themselves outwardly as skin and hair coat disorders. Therefore, by routinely inspecting your pet you are more likely to discover these problems early, which could, in itself, be lifesaving.

Question 2: *How often should I groom my pet?*

Dogs and cats should be brushed daily to help remove dirt and dead hair. This daily brushing will stimulate the production of natural skin oils and help spread them throughout the hair coat, thereby keeping it shiny and lustrous. Try to devote five to ten minutes daily to this task.

As far as bathing is concerned, pets with normal, healthy skin and coats need only be bathed "as needed." Use your judgment on this. When your indoor pet begins to smell like an outdoor pet or starts to accumulate dirt or dandruff, it is probably bath time! Beware though: Bathing a healthy dog or cat too frequently, especially with the wrong type of shampoo, could remove natural oils and predispose your pet to dry skin and related skin problems. For animals with normal skin that require more frequent bathing (that is, more than twice per month), you should use only hypoallergenic or soap-free products when shampooing.

If your dog or cat suffers from skin parasites, such as fleas and ticks, or from such skin ailments as allergies or seborrhea, the bathing frequency will probably need to be increased. During flea season it may be necessary to bathe a pet weekly, using a safe flea and tick shampoo. If your pet is suffering from a skin infection, your veterinarian may prescribe daily baths with a medicated shampoo. Now you may ask, "But didn't you say that bathing my pet so often will dry out his skin?" I did indeed, but I was referring to those healthy pets not affected with skin problems. For dogs and cats with skin disease, the benefits of properly treating such a condition far outweigh the risks associated with dry skin. Furthermore, properly formulated medicated shampoos prescribed by your veterinarian should moisturize, not dry out, the skin, even with daily bathing.

In addition to brushing and bathing, your pet's ears, eyes, teeth, and nails will also require periodic attention. By giving your dog or cat a mini-physical examination weekly, you will be able to assess your pet's health and grooming status (see page 35). Be sure to use the examination checklist provided for this purpose and, if indicated, perform any specific grooming task at that time.

Question 3: *I've heard that cats don't need as much grooming as dogs. Is that true?*

While it is true that most cats are more efficient at grooming themselves than are dogs, this does not exclude them from grooming. There are some differences between the two species that bear noting.

Because they do quite well at keeping themselves groomed, cats almost never need routine cleansing baths. Thank goodness, since as a general rule, most cats do not care to be bathed! Since healthy cats have these meticulous grooming habits, an unkempt, greasy hair coat should alert you that your cat may be ill and needs to be examined by a veterinarian.

Feline skin is thinner and, in many cases, much more sensitive than canine skin. As a result, greater gen-

tleness and care must be taken when brushing, combing, or removing mats to prevent injury or irritation to the skin surface. Because cats are so efficient at grooming themselves, you might think that cats hardly ever need brushing. This isn't true. One excellent reason for brushing your cat regularly is to reduce the incidence of gastrointestinal upset due to hairballs. It does not matter whether a cat has short or long hair, hairballs can still develop. Furthermore, if fleas, which are known carriers of tapeworms, happen to be ingested along with the strands of hair during self-grooming, your cat could develop a tapeworm infestation. As you can see, brushing your cat on a regular basis is important not only for aesthetic reasons, but for medical reasons as well.

Though cats are skilled groomers, they still need your help.

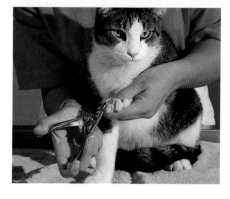

The toenails of cats are more fragile than those of dogs.

Many shampoos, sprays, and chemicals used commonly and harmlessly on dogs can be toxic and deadly to cats. For example, products containing tar or salicylic acid (aspirin) can be highly toxic to felines if ingested (and keep in mind that cats love to lick themselves, especially after bathing). You must also exercise caution when applying flea and tick insecticides that contain organophosphates because side effects of these particular chemicals are seen more frequently in cats than in dogs.

The toenails of cats are more fragile than those of their canine counterparts, therefore you must take extra care when trimming them. Be certain the nail clippers you use are sharp to avoid splintering or cracking a nail.

Ear infections are less common in cats than in some dogs, mainly because their ears stand erect. This does not mean that you should neglect this aspect of grooming, however. Always use a drying agent in the ears after bathing and be on the lookout for signs of ear mites or other problems (see "Ear Care," page 34).

Of course, there are many other differences, but the benefits afforded by grooming remain the same regardless of the species involved.

Chapter 2

Understanding Your Pet's Skin and Coat

To help you better understand the importance of grooming and the origin of many skin and coat problems, I am going to introduce you to some basic information concerning the normal anatomy and physiology of the skin and hair. Don't worry: I won't go into great detail, and you may be surprised at what you will learn!

The Skin

The skin is made up of three layers: the *epidermis* (outer layer), the *dermis* (middle layer), and the *hypodermis* (inner layer). Dogs have thinner skin than humans; cats' skin is even thinner. Regardless of the species, the layers of the skin act collectively to perform many important functions. Three of these include protection, temperature regulation, and storage.

Protection

The skin protects the body from outside trauma. It also helps maintain the internal environment by preventing the loss of water and nutrients. Glands within the skin (sebaceous glands) secrete oils that lubricate the skin and hair, and also protect against bacterial and fungal infections. The skin of cats and dogs is less acidic than that of humans. As a result, many soaps and shampoos designed for humans can actually irritate and dry out the skin of a pet, even after one use. To be safe, use only those shampoos formulated for use on dogs and cats. An inappropriate shampoo can cripple the skin's protective capabilities.

Because dogs cannot sweat, panting is an important part of their thermoregulation.

Temperature Regulation

The skin helps to regulate body temperature and protects against rapid temperature changes, both hot and cold, through the use of hair, blood vessels, and fat. Dogs and cats can't "sweat" like humans do, so they need to use other methods to keep the body from overheating. Panting is one method you are probably familiar with; another is to trigger an increased flow of blood to the skin to release heat. The hair coat and fatty tissue within and under the skin effectively act as insulation against both heat and cold. One mistake pet owners often make is to shave short the coat of a long-haired dog during the summer months, thinking that this will make the dog cooler and more comfortable. In actuality, the lack of this insulating hair could overburden the skin's ability to regulate temperature and increase susceptibility to heat stroke. When shaving your pet for the summer, don't be too liberal in your clipping. More important, provide plenty of shade and plenty of fresh water during the hot months.

Storage

The skin is an ideal reservoir for fat, water, vitamins, proteins, and other nutrients. By serving this function, it also acts as a reliable indicator in the event that a deficiency in any of these items occurs, thereby alerting pet owners to potential health problems early.

If skin integrity is lost, or if a skin disease strikes, your pet could be in for a lot of trouble simply because these vital functions will be disrupted. Never ignore a skin problem, no matter how trivial it may seem. You may be seeing just the tip of the iceberg!

The Hair Coat

The coats of dogs and cats come in a variety of lengths, textures, and colors, all of which are largely determined by breed and family genetics. Both species have a primary outercoat, made up of hairs called "guard hairs," and a secondary undercoat, consisting of much finer, denser "wool hairs." These wool hairs tend to be much more prominent in cats than in dogs. Long, firm tactile hairs (or whiskers) are found on the head of both species. As far as hair length is concerned, cats basically have either long or short hair, while dogs can have either short, medium, or long hair.

The color of the coat is directly proportional to the amount of pigment contained within the individual hairs themselves. For instance, hairs lacking pigment are white in color, whereas those with an overabundance of pigment are black. Between these two extremes, different levels of pigmentation exist, each producing a unique coat color.

Unlike people, whose hair grows continuously, both canines and felines have hair that grows in cycles. This cyclical growth is responsible for the phenomenon we all know as "shedding." Each hair cycle consists of three phases: *anagen* (the growing period), *catagen* (the transitional period), and *telogen* (the resting period). It is in this latter stage, telogen, that the hairs die and are soon shed. Hair cycles occur in a mosaic pattern: neighboring hair follicles are in different stages of the hair cycle at any one time, so many cycles are going on at once in your pet's coat. Thank goodness, otherwise your pet would go bald with each shedding cycle!

Now you may ask "What about those dogs that supposedly don't shed at all?" Some people claim that certain breeds, such as poodles and terriers, have hairs that grow continuously, and therefore do not shed. Whether or not this is indeed the case, or if it is simply that these breeds have extended hair cycles, is still a matter of speculation. Until proven otherwise, it is safe to assume that all dogs undergo hair cycles and will at one time or another shed their hair.

The hair cycle and shedding can be influenced by a number of factors, such as nutrition, disease, environmental temperature, pregnancy, etc. Clipping or shaving can cause the hair to enter into telogen and, in some cases, remain there for a long time (see "Hair Loss Not Related to Disease," page 113). This may explain why hair that is removed for a surgical procedure sometimes requires a long time to grow back. Stress can also be a big influence; that's why you will often see dogs and cats shed profusely at the veterinary office (see

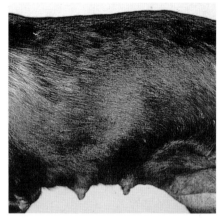

The hair cycle can be influenced by a number of factors, including pregnancy.

"telogen effluvium," page 114). Some experts feel that stress-related shedding is actually a defense mechanism designed to leave an adversary with a mouthful (or handful) of hair if he chooses to attack.

Neither stress nor any of the other conditions mentioned above actually control the hair cycle; they merely influence it. Instead, this control is exerted by seasonal changes in the photoperiod, or length of daylight. If you consider the way nature intended it, increased shedding should occur during the spring and the fall, thus helping the animal adapt to the temperature extremes to be faced during the upcoming summer or winter months. However, since many pets are kept indoors at least part of the time and are thus exposed to constant degrees of artificial light, nature's rule will not hold true for them. Instead, much to the dismay of their owners, these pets often shed year-round, despite seasonal changes.

Chapter 3

Nutrition for a Healthy Skin and Coat

The old adage, "You are what you eat," holds true for dogs and cats. A well-balanced diet is essential for a strong immune system and healthy skin and hair coat (see the table on page 21). Because skin, hair, and nails are in a dynamic state of growth, they constantly require large amounts of nutrients. If a nutritional deficiency is present, these are the first areas in which it usually shows up. Let's take a look at some essential nutrient groups and find out why they are so important to the integument (the skin, hair, and nails).

Proteins and Amino Acids

Proteins and their components, the amino acids, are organic compounds found throughout the body. Their function is to serve as the structural elements for cells, enzymes, hormones, antibodies, and a host of other vital constituents. Though the body has the capability of manufacturing most of the specific amino acids and proteins that it needs, it cannot do this without the proper fuel. Where does this fuel come from? It comes from food.

Did you know that up to 30 percent of the daily protein requirement in dogs and cats can be used for the replacement of dead skin and hair? It's easy to see that proteins play a vital role in maintaining the integrity of these regions. Deficiencies can arise either from rations that are low in protein or contain a poor source of protein. Disease conditions such as parasitism or malnutrition can also rob the body of proteins. Signs of protein deficiency can include a dry, rough, thin coat, with or without bald spots (due to lack of hair replacement); flaky skin; and abnormal shedding cycles.

Adult dogs and cats need, respectively, at least 16 percent and 20 percent of their daily energy as protein; puppies and kittens, nursing mothers, and pregnant pets need even higher levels. Most commercial dog and cat foods satisfy these requirements;

Good nutrition is essential for healthy skin and hair.

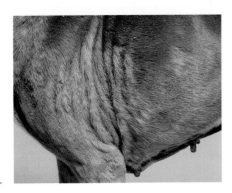

Fatty acid deficiencies can cause hair loss and dry, thickened skin.

however, not all are the same. Choose a ration that contains protein from more than one food source to ensure that your pet receives a well-balanced blend of amino acids and proteins. Contrary to popular belief, dog foods labeled as "high protein" are not necessary to achieve a luxurious coat. In fact, many researchers feel that such a diet fed long-term to your dog could seriously impair kidney function. As a result, always consult your veterinarian before putting your dog on such a diet.

Fatty Acids

If your pet has a dry, lackluster coat, or dry, flaky skin, a fatty acid deficiency may be the culprit. Fatty acids are the compounds that combine to make oils, fats, and fatty tissue within the body. Along with providing an important source of energy for their host, they are also vital for healthy skin and hair.

Fatty acids are important components of the oily secretions found normally on the skin and coats of healthy dogs and cats. These oils serve to retain water, thereby keeping the skin moisturized and the hair coat soft. Most fatty acids are manufactured inside the body; certain others are considered "essential"—that is, they cannot be manufactured by the body and must be supplied through the diet. Linoleic acid is an essential fatty acid required by dogs, whereas linoleic acid and arachidonic acid are needed by cats. Most commercial foods have adequate quantities of these; however, deficiencies can occur in dry foods if they are stored over a long period of time (greater than six months).

Many pet owners add corn oil, vegetable oil, or other sources of fat to their pet's diet to supplement these fatty acids. One-half to one teaspoon per twenty pounds daily of one of these supplements usually is sufficient. While there is certainly nothing wrong with using one of these, you should watch closely to be sure that the supplement does not cause stomach upset or diarrhea in your pet. Furthermore, since many vitamins and minerals are important for the proper utilization of these fats, you should consider a balanced vitamin-mineral supplement at the same time. If all this seems like too much trouble, seriously consider using one of the many nutritional supplements for the skin and coat that can be found on the market today. Since these are formulated to contain a well-balanced mixture of amino acids, fatty acids, vitamins, and minerals, you can be assured that they will work as well, if not better, than most "home remedies." If interested, ask your veterinarian to recommend one for your pet.

The use of select fatty acids as anti-inflammatory weapons against the itchy effects of allergies in pets just recently has come to light. Research has revealed that certain fatty acids derived from cold water fish oil may have the profound ability to incorporate within and divert the pathway leading to inflammation and itching in dogs. When used concurrently with other forms of medication or therapy, such as antihistamines, vitamins, and antibiotics, they often provide a safe and effective alternative to the old therapeutic standby for itchy dogs, steroids. Consult your veterinarian for more details.

Vitamins and Minerals

Probably the most misunderstood of all dietary substances, vitamins and minerals are required for normal metabolic and enzyme system function within the body. Many pet owners claim that certain of these substances, when taken in large enough quantities, can repel fleas and even cure feline leukemia in cats. Though claims such as these are farfetched, vitamins and minerals can indeed offer therapeutic benefits for select disorders in pets, especially those involving the integument, when used under veterinary supervision.

A teaspoon of corn oil can be added to the food to supplement the fatty acids in the diet.

The vitamins of most importance to the skin and coat of dogs and cats include the B vitamins (including thiamine, riboflavin, niacin, etc.), vitamin A (the retinoids), and vitamin E.

The water-soluble B vitamins are necessary for the effective metabolism of proteins, fats, and carbohydrates within the body, and the incorporation of these substances into the integument. As a result, deficiencies in one or more of these vitamins can have profound effects. The coat often becomes thin and fragile, and loses its luster. Hair loss can also occur as the skin becomes dry, scaly,

Most commercial pet foods available today provide well-balanced nutrition.

and thickened. Once such a deficiency is recognized, supplementation can be used to reverse the symptoms. The notion that these vitamins, when fed in large quantities, are effective at repelling fleas is entirely without foundation.

Vitamin A, a fat-soluble vitamin, belongs to a group of compounds known as *retinoids*. These substances are vital to the integument. Among other things, retinoids regulate metabolism and growth within epithelial tissue. Retinoid deficiencies can create marked changes in the skin. Such deficiencies leave the skin thickened, greasy, scaly, and highly prone to infection. Retinoids have been used for years in human medicine to treat a variety of skin ailments, yet only recently has attention turned to their use in dogs and cats. Conditions such as canine seborrhea have been successfully treated in a limited number of cases using one or more of these compounds, yet their full therapeutic potential still remains unknown. One thing is for certain: the indiscriminate use of vitamin A and other retinoids can cause serious toxicity problems, including bone disease. As a result, supplementation should be performed only under the supervision of a veterinarian.

Vitamin E is another important vitamin that helps maintain the integrity and function of all body cells, including those of the skin. In addition, it helps guard against inflammation and protects fats from becoming rancid. The significance of this latter function is characterized by the fact that, as far as the skin and hair coat are concerned, a deficiency of vitamin E looks strikingly similar to a fatty acid deficiency. Even though a naturally occurring deficiency of vitamin E in pets is rare, it can happen if they are fed rations that have been stored over an extended period of time, or if fed diets that contain large amounts of polyunsaturated fatty acids. In regard to the therapeutic uses of vitamin E, it has been medically employed to combat inflammation, demodectic mange, and immune-mediated skin diseases in dogs and cats. Its anti-inflammatory effects in dogs suffering from allergies appear to be of little consequence when used as a sole means of treatment; however, combining vitamin E supplementation with other treatment modalities may improve its effectiveness. Because vitamin E, like vitamin A, is a fat-soluble vitamin, toxicity could result if too much is given at one time. Therefore, as with vitamin A supplementation, give vitamin E to pets only upon your veterinarian's approval.

Minerals differ from vitamins in that they are inorganic compounds, whereas vitamins are organic, or carbon-containing. The function of minerals is similar to that of their organic counterparts. As with vitamins, minerals are key components of numerous enzyme systems and compounds within the body. With regard to the skin and coat, one mineral in particular seems to stand out among the rest: zinc. It is important for protein, fat, and carbohydrate utilization, and deficiencies of this trace mineral can cause dull, dry coats; hair loss; and greasy, thickened skin. As with other nutrients, naturally occurring deficiencies in zinc are rare in pets fed quality, well-balanced rations. However, deficiencies can occur in those pets fed calcium supplements (for example, mothers nursing newborn pups), since calcium can interfere with the absorption of zinc from within the gastrointestinal tract. In addition, a genetically based zinc-deficiency syndrome has been recognized in breeds such as Alaskan malamutes and Siberian huskies. In these instances, inadequate absorption of zinc from the gastrointestinal tract or inadequate zinc metabolism once absorption takes place is to blame. Fortunately for these dogs, zinc supplementation can be used to overcome this problem and help treat the skin disorders that resulted from the original deficiency.

As you can see, vitamins and minerals are required for healthy skin and hair. However, they should never be used indiscriminately to treat skin disorders. Giving large amounts of one particular vitamin or mineral could actually lead to a deficiency of another (for example, the relationship between zinc and calcium), or could lead to a severe toxic reaction. If you insist on supplementing your pet's diet, be sure to use only a supplement that contains the proper balance of vitamins and minerals.

Important Nutrients for the Skin and Coat

Nutrient	Importance	Signs of Deficiency
Dietary protein and amino acids	Precursors for developing skin and hair	Thin, dry, fragile coat; scaly skin
Dietary fats & fatty acids	Natural components of hair, skin, and oily secretions; anti-inflammatory properties	Dull, dry coat; hair loss; scaly, thickened skin
B vitamins	Protein, fat, and carbohydrate metabolism	Similar to protein and fat deficiencies
Vitamin A	Regulates metabolism in epithelial tissue	Thick, scaly skin; skin infections
Vitamin E	Protects cell membranes; protects fats from rancidity	Similar to fatty acid deficiency; inflammation
Zinc	Component of many enzyme systems; affects protein utilization	Dull, dry coats; crusty skin; hair loss; thickened foot pads

Chapter 4
Basic Home Grooming Techniques

A Word About Safety

Grooming should be a pleasant and safe experience, both for you and your pet. The last thing you want is a rambunctious animal hindering your efforts, thereby endangering itself and you. This is why it is imperative that

Any successful grooming program starts with proper training.

dogs and cats are taught at an early age to accept grooming as part of their normal routine and to behave properly during grooming sessions.

If a pet objects to any type of handling, it could be due to:

• lack of obedience training;
• fear of the procedure;
• pain associated with the procedure.

Let us examine each of these situations a little more closely.

Obedience training in dogs should be started as early as eight weeks of age. Since this is when true memory begins, it is one of the easiest times to train dogs; the first things they learn tend to stick with them for a lifetime. Get yourself a good book on obedience training (such as Ted Baer's *Communicating with Your Dog*, Barron's Educational Series) and devote time to this task. It will save you a lot of headaches in the future! For grooming purposes, your dog should be well versed in the meaning of the commands *stay, sit,* and *down*. Any number of different training techniques can be used; just remember to keep the initial training sessions short and *never* use any type of physical punishment on a puppy between the ages of eight and 16 weeks. Physically punishing young puppies can cause permanent behavioral problems that usually worsen as they mature. Instead of punishing for a mistake, use lots, and I mean *lots*, of praise for a job well done.

It's a proven fact that pups respond favorably to this, ensuring quicker and more satisfactory training results.

As far as cats are concerned, obedience training is a bit more challenging, yet not impossible. Again, there are books available that go into the various and sometimes subtle aspects

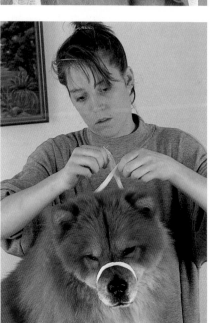

If your dog resists during essential procedures... an improvised muzzle may be necessary. This one is tied with rolled bandage gauze (left). Start with the bandage below the jaw; tie a knot on the bridge of the nose; cross the ends below the jaw; and finish off with a knot on the back of the neck. Do not tie too tightly!

Two methods of restraining cats (right).

of feline obedience training, and I encourage you to get one.

Fear can play a role in problem behaviors that may arise while grooming. A good example of this is the cat that fears running water. Though you may not be able to eliminate such fears completely, you can certainly take steps to lessen them. For instance, fill that tub with water first, before bringing your pet into the room. Also, turn on the clippers well away from the pet and let it get used to the sound before actually clipping. One of the best ways to avoid "fear syndromes" is to introduce grooming procedures and grooming utensils to your pet at an early age, preferably no later than 12 weeks. Above all, make sure these first experiences are nothing but positive.

Keep the initial grooming sessions short, and allow your pet to investigate and become accustomed to the equipment you are using beforehand. Once again, using lots of praise for good behavior.

Finally, pain will turn even the most obedient, fearless Dr. Jekyll into a snapping and scratching Mr. Hyde. If you are using the correct instruments and methods, pain should rarely be a component of your grooming program. However, even with the right instruments and methods, it sometimes becomes a factor, especially if inflammation or infection is present. If a procedure is going to be painful to your pet, do not proceed with it! This is a job for your veterinarian.

The bottom line is this: Use common sense when it comes to safety and use proper restraint when needed (see page 23). If your pet starts to threaten you with teeth or nails, regardless of reason, abort what you are doing immediately. Again, in these cases, let your veterinarian or professional groomer perform those procedures over which your pet absolutely throws a fuss. Not only will this prevent injuries, but it will spare both you and your reluctant pet much mental anguish and despair.

Equipment and Supplies

To make your job easier, equip yourself with the right type of grooming tools and products. Don't worry about spending lots of money; the basics will do just fine. You must be sure, however, that the tools or products you choose match your pet's particular needs. The following list includes some of the essentials that could go into a typical home grooming kit.

Brush
Comb
Scissors
Clippers (optional)
Nail trimmers/clotting powder
Ear cleanser-dryer
Protective eye ointment
Tooth brush/dentifrice
Cotton balls/swabs
Hypoallergenic shampoo
Insecticidal dip (optional)
Coat conditioner/moisturizer
Towels/blow dryer

These grooming supplies should be easy to come by. Sources include pet supply stores, pet shops, grooming salons, department stores, veterinary offices, and dog or cat shows. Certain mail order houses also offer grooming supplies at good prices. Check your favorite dog or cat magazine for advertisements offering supplies at discount.

One piece of equipment not mentioned in the above list is a grooming table. In reality, any table or shelf will suffice (even the floor will do!) just so long as it does not have a slippery surface. If it does, you can easily make the surface nonslip by placing a rubber bath mat on top of it. Covering the surface in some manner will also prevent it from getting scratched by toenails.

Brushes

It's incredible how many different types of brushes you have to choose from for your pet. It is essential that you choose the right one, because inappropriate brushes could actually

Recommendations for Brushing

Type of Hair Coat	Type of Brush	Direction of Brushing
Short, smooth coats (most retrievers, hounds, Chihuahuas, etc.; short-haired cats)	Soft to medium bristle brush short, closely spaced bristles	With the grain of the coat
Short, wiry coats (terriers, etc.)	Firm bristle brush with short, closely spaced bristles; slicker brush	With the grain of the coat
Medium to long, flowing coats (golden retrievers, Lhasa Apso, spaniels, setters, etc.; long-haired cats)	Soft to medium bristle brush with long, medium to wide-spaced bristles; wire pin brush; slicker brush for mats and tangles	With the grain of the coat
Harsh outer coats with soft, woolly undercoats (sheepdog, collies, shepherds, Chow Chows, Pomeranians, etc.)	Firm bristle brush with long, wide-spaced bristles; wire pin brush; slicker brush for tangles and mats	Outer coat—with the grain; Undercoat—against the grain
Thin, delicate coats (Yorkshire terrier, Maltese)	Wire pin brush; soft slicker brush for tangles and mats	Gentle, delicate strokes with and against the grain to prevent damage to the coat

Your favorite pet store or supply house should carry those products and supplies needed for home grooming.

damage your pet's coat. Use the table on page 25 to help you make the right choice.

Bristle brushes come in a variety of shapes and textures and can be used on all types of coats. Generally speaking, the longer the hair coat, the more widely spaced and longer the bristles on the brush should be. In addition, the coarser the coat, the stiffer those bristles need to be. For example, a cat with long, silky hair would benefit most from using a soft bristled brush with bristles that are moderately to widely spaced. Conversely, a wire-haired terrier with short,

Be sure to select the right brush for your pet's individual needs.

coarse hair would require a stiff bristled brush with the bristles spaced closely together.

Wire-pin brushes are favored by many groomers for use on dogs with medium to long hair, or on those with woolly or curly coats. Long-haired cats can also benefit from this type of brush, but some cats will object to its use. As with any brush, it should be applied using full, gentle strokes to prevent breaking or damaging the hair.

Slicker brushes contain numerous fine wire bristles that are usually embedded within a square or rectangular backing. These are especially useful in removing snarls, tangles, and mats, as well as dense, shed undercoats. Some groomers even use slicker brushes for fluff drying (see "Drying," page 52). Use these brushes with care, because if used improperly they could do more harm than good.

For general care and upkeep of your brush, regardless of the type, remove the hair that has accumulated on its surface after each brushing. Get a new brush if bristles are missing, or if it doesn't seem to be doing the job anymore. It's also a good idea to disinfect the brush every so often with a germicidal spray. Rinse the brush off thoroughly before using again.

Combs

Like brushes, combs come in a number of sizes and shapes, each designed for a specific type of coat. The amount of space between the teeth determines which comb should

There are a number of different brushes and combs from which to choose. Clockwise from top: two types of wire-pin brushes, three types of bristle brushes, two types of slicker brushes, dematting comb, flea comb, stripping comb, wide-toothed comb, combination comb.

be used on which coat. For example, combs with fine teeth spaced closely together are useful for dogs with short coats and for short- and long-haired cats; the wide-toothed combs are better for dogs with medium to long hair. Special combs, such as stripping combs, are useful for removing or "stripping" dead hair from the longer coats; rubber curry combs are effective at massaging the skin and removing dead hair from short-haired breeds. Regardless of the type used, follow these guidelines when combing:

- Use a comb only after you've given your pet a thorough brushing.
- In order to gain full benefit when using a comb, always insert the comb to its full depth into the coat.
- Never force a comb through hair. To do so could severely damage a hair coat, not to mention the discomfort it would cause your pet.

- Replace all combs that have broken or missing teeth.

Scissors

A pair of scissors, preferably blunt-tipped, can be helpful in removing loosely adhered mats and foreign objects from the coat. Unless you are planning on doing some advanced cosmetic grooming, you needn't invest in expensive grooming shears. Even a pair of child's safety scissors will work just fine in most instances. Care and

For general purpose use, a pair of scissors with rounded ends is ideal.

27

upkeep of your scissors consists of cleaning them after each use, and replacing them if ever the two blades fail to cut effectively.

Clippers

If you want to get into more advanced cosmetic grooming techniques, you will need to purchase a good pair of clippers. (You may want to get a set anyway, since these can come in quite handy for working out a matted coat.) Oster Model A5 clippers are an excellent choice for home grooming purposes. Oster clipper blades come in different sizes for specialized uses. The table on page 77

A good set of clippers is a must for advanced grooming techniques.

explains the differences between these blades in greater detail. For basic home grooming techniques, the #10 and the #40 blade are satisfactory for most tasks. The #10 can be used to remove most mats and to perform minor trimming, while the #40, which clips all the way down to the skin, may be needed for tough mats or for clipping and exposing skin lesions or infections. If you plan on performing advanced clipping procedures, such as those presented in the section entitled "Advanced Cosmetic Grooming Techniques," pages 57-61, you will need other blades as well. Refer to that section for more details.

Since a set of quality clippers and blades is not cheap, you will want to be sure to take good care of them. After each use, the blades should be washed, disassembled, and oiled using blade wash, lubricating oil, and spray disinfectant. Follow the manufacturer's instructions concerning cleaning and blade disassembly. During use, stop periodically to brush away hair and debris that may have accumulated on the exposed blade and clipper surfaces. Be sure to keep the blades well lubricated and cool during use by employing a product such as Oster's "Kool Lube" Lubricant at periodic intervals during the clipping procedure.

If you notice any teeth missing from your clipper blades, it's time for new ones. Damaged blades can scratch or lacerate the skin surface and predispose it to infection. Similarly, dull blades can cause clipper burn by pull-

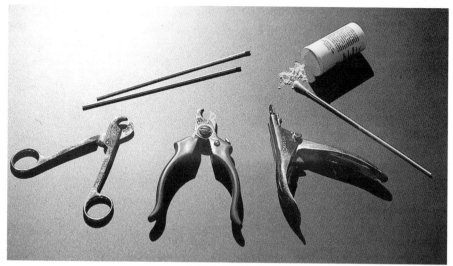

An assortment of nail accessories.

ing hair from the hair follicles instead of neatly cutting it. Dull blades should be either replaced or sharpened before using again.

As far as the clipper assembly itself, little maintenance is usually required. Oiling, greasing, and brush replacement may become necessary at times. Refer to your owner's manual for more details.

Finally, as with any electrical appliance, *never* operate your clippers around water (and there may be plenty lying about if you have just bathed your pet). Also, never use clippers on a wet animal because of the danger of electrical shock.

Nail Accessories

Nail accessories include a good pair of toenail trimmers, and some clotting powder—just in case! There are many types of nail trimmers to choose from, including guillotine trimmers, scissor or plier trimmers, and, of course, the old-fashioned human nail clippers. The latter should be reserved for only very small dogs, puppies, and kittens, whereas the other types will work on just about any size animal. Avoid using the human nail clippers on the nails of adult cats, for these could splinter or shatter the nail. Regardless of the type used, always be sure that the blade surfaces remain sharp to avoid pulling or twisting the nail. One advantage that the guillotine trimmer has over the others is that its blade can be replaced inexpensively when dull.

Ear Cleansers and Drying Agents

As you will see later, ear cleansers and drying agents are a must for all pet owners. Pet ear cleansers come in a variety of types and ingredients. A

A general purpose ear cleanser is a must for every home grooming kit.

good one should clean the ear by dissolving and emulsifying the excess wax and debris within the canal, and should dry the ear canal at the same time. This product can be obtained from your veterinarian or pet supplier. As alternatives, isopropyl alcohol or hydrogen peroxide can be used, but the cleaning action of these is less than that of an ear cleanser, and they also may irritate and sting inflamed ear canals.

Ophthalmic Ointment or Drops

Whenever you bathe dogs and cats or use chemicals around their face, always protect their eyes before doing so. Even those products touting "no tears" can severely burn the surface of

Applying a sterile ophthalmic ointment is the preferred method of eye protection.

the eye if present in strong enough concentrations. Many people advocate the use of mineral oil in the eyes, but I prefer a sterile ophthalmic ointment. The advantages are two-fold. First, ointments provide a much thicker protective film over the surface of the eyes than do drops. Second, you do not run the risk of contaminating the eyes with a non-sterile preparation. You can obtain one of these sterile ointments from pet stores, pharmacies, or your veterinarian.

Dental Accessories

To help your pet maintain clean teeth and fresh breath, equip yourself with a soft-bristled toothbrush (any style will do) and a specially formulated pet dentifrice. Before you laugh at the thought of brushing your pet's teeth, just think of what your teeth would be like if you never brushed them! Clean teeth are very important in relation to your pet's overall health (see "Dental Care" page 41). Pet dentifrices come in either a paste or liquid form. These can be found just about anywhere pet supplies are sold, and are the preferred choices over such old standbys as baking soda and human toothpastes. Human preparations should be avoided if at all possible, since these can upset your pet's stomach if swallowed.

You may have seen manual dental scalers in pet stores or heard of pet owners using these instruments at home to scrape the tartar off their pet's teeth. I highly discourage such use for two reasons. First, these instruments are rarely effective at removing tartar where it really counts—up under the gum line. Trying to do so on a nonsedated dog or cat can lead to severe injury to yourself or your pet. Second, if you scale the teeth without also polishing them afterwards, you are defeating the purpose. Scaling creates little nicks and etches in the tooth enamel that, unless polished smooth again, will act as a site for plaque and tartar buildup, this time even faster than before.

Cotton Balls and Swabs

Keep plenty of cotton balls and swabs handy to clean around the eyes and ears. You can also use them when expressing anal sacs. Cotton balls can be placed in the outer ears before bathing to keep out moisture. Never stick anything deep into the ear canal, especialy cotton swabs. This probing will push debris further down into the ear and can do great damage to the ear drum.

Shampoos

The three most common grooming errors I see pet owners commit in regard to shampoos for their pets are:

- Using a shampoo formulated for human use
- Using a medicated shampoo without having the pet's skin condition diagnosed by a veterinarian
- Using dog shampoos on cats

Remember, bathing is only necessary if the skin and coat are dirty or if a medical condition exists. In fact, frequent brushing and combing are

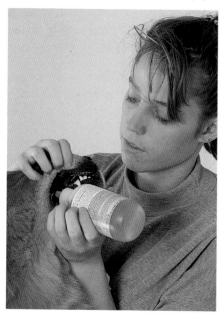

Believe it or not, there is such thing as "pet mouthwash."

probably the most important things you can do to keep your pet clean. However, if a cleanup bath is indicated, there are many excellent cleansing shampoos available that will do the job gently and effectively. The brand you use isn't as important as the formulation (although many do a better job than others). Avoid human

Read all labels carefully.

shampoos and preparations because these can be too acidic for your dog or cat's skin, and often do more harm than good. Instead, look for one that is formulated especially for dogs and cats. If your pet likes to roll around in the flower bed and you are having to resort to the bath one or more times weekly, consider refining your choice even more by using a soap-free hypoallergenic shampoo. There are many good ones on the market to choose from, and your veterinarian will be able to recommend one for you. Select a shampoo that contains plenty of moisturizers and conditioners. Alternatively, you can apply a moisturizer during the rinse or after bathing (see below).

If your dog or cat has a white coat, consider using a shampoo that contains a bluing agent (this will usually

Active Ingredients of Medicated Shampoos

Ingredient	Actions	Comments
Tar (coal tar)	Antiseborrheic; relieves itching; degreaser; anti-inflammatory	Can be toxic to cats unless highly refined; unpleasant odor
Sulfur	Antiseborrheic, antifungal, antibacterial; relieves itching	Often combined with tar for additive effects
Salicylic acid	Antiseborrheic, anti-inflammatory	Can be toxic to cats
Selenium	Antiseborrheic, antibacterial; drying agent	—
Benzoyl peroxide	Antibacterial, antiseborrheic; relieves itching; degreaser	Can be irritating to the skin; may bleach colored fabrics and clothes
Chlorhexidine	Antibacterial; antifungal	Effective against ringworm; safe for cats
Triclosan	Antibacterial	—
Iodine	Antibacterial, antifungal	Effective against ringworm; can be toxic to cats
Lanolin, oils, fatty alcohols, glycerol esters	Emollients	Soothe and soften the skin
Propylene glycol, urea, glycerin	Moisturizers	Add moisture to the epidermis
Aluminum acetate, silver nitrate, tannic acid	Drying agents	Good for moist skin lesions

be indicated on the label). Bluing is also available at your grocery store and can be added directly to the rinse water. The end result of either method will be a whiter, brighter coat.

If your pet has a skin condition and you believe a medicated shampoo might help, the first step is to consult your veterinarian. You should use a medicated shampoo only under the supervision of your veterinarian. Despite good intentions, blindly selecting a medicated shampoo when you are not familiar with the chemical involved could adversely affect your pet. The table on page 32 lists the ingredients commonly found in many of the medicated shampoos pre-scribed for dogs and cats, and their indications.

Dips

Dips are useful when something more effective than a flea shampoo or spray is needed to control fleas and ticks on a pet. Because certain dips can be toxic not only to pets but also to the persons administering the dip, it is imperative that the manufacturer's label directions are followed precisely. For more information on dips, see "Bathing and Dipping," page 47.

Coat Conditioners, Moisturizers, and Emollients

Skin and coat conditioners are designed to lubricate skin surfaces and to help prevent tangles and mats from forming within the coat. They also help to replace the natural oils lost from the skin and hair due to bath-

Coat conditioner sprays can be used between baths.

ing and disease. These oils act as moisturizers by helping to retain mois-ture next to the skin, thereby leaving the skin and coat soft and supple. Emollients are substances that soothe and soften the skin surface. They have been proven to be helpful if the skin is especially sensitive or irritated. Most after-bath products found at a pet store will contain a combination of conditioners, moisturizers, and/or emollients. For best results, choose a rinse for after bathing (when the skin is still moist), and a spray for between baths. Note, however, that if your pet has a skin disorder, such as a moist hot spot, you should consult your vet-erinarian before using any after-bath product. In many cases of skin dis-ease, you must actually dry out the affected area rather than seal in mois-ture (see "Hot Spots," page 98).

Specific Techniques

Giving Your Pet an At-Home Physical Examination

As mentioned previously, grooming sessions provide the ideal opportunity to assess the health status of your pet.

Mini-examinations are quick and easy to perform, and can be very effective in the early detection of health problems, before they become well established. Examine your pet at least once a week, using the checklist provided on page 35 as a guide. An abnormal finding should prompt you to contact your veterinarian to obtain a professional evaluation. Also remember that these home examinations are no substitute for routine veterinary checkups, which should be performed at least annually.

Ear Care

Approximately seven out of ten dogs and cats that I see in daily practice have dirty ears. Many of these pets also have infections brewing in those ears. For this reason, preventive ear care for all dogs and cats is essential. By keeping the ears clean and dry, you can thwart potential problems right from the start, before they become chronic.

Let's begin by reviewing some basic anatomical features of the canine and feline ear. The ear flaps, or *pinnae*, are

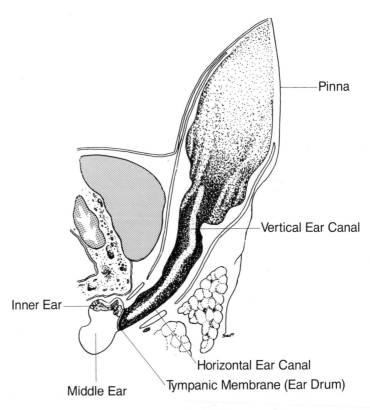

Pinna

Vertical Ear Canal

Inner Ear

Horizontal Ear Canal

Middle Ear

Tympanic Membrane (Ear Drum)

The Canine Ear

The Physical Exam

General Evaluation

_____ Alert
_____ Active
_____ Good appetite
_____ Abnormal posture*
_____ Lameness*

_____ Weak*
_____ Lethargic*
_____ Poor appetite*
_____ Weight loss/gain*

Skin and Hair Coat

_____ Appears normal
_____ Hair loss
_____ Dull
_____ Scaly
_____ Dry
_____ Oily
_____ Itching

_____ Shedding
_____ Mats
_____ Tumors or warts
_____ Infection
_____ Abnormal lumps
_____ Infection
_____ Parasites

Eyes

_____ Appear normal
_____ Discharge
_____ Redness
_____ Eyelid abnormalities
_____ Squinting

_____ Infection
_____ Unequal pupils
_____ Cloudiness
_____ Discoloration

Ears

_____ Appear normal
_____ Inflamed
_____ Itchy
_____ Discharge
_____ Head shaking

_____ Parasites
_____ Bad odor
_____ Tumors
_____ Excessive hair
_____ Head tilt

Nose and Throat

_____ Appear normal
_____ Nasal discharge

_____ Enlarged lymph nodes
_____ Dry, crusty nose

Mouth, Teeth, and Gums

_____ Appear normal
_____ Broken teeth
_____ Retained baby teeth
_____ Tartar build-up
_____ Tumors

_____ Loose teeth
_____ Gingivitis
_____ Excess salivation
_____ Pale gums
_____ Ulcers

Miscellaneous

_____ Tense/painful abdomen
_____ Coughing/wheezing
_____ Abnormal stools
_____ Abnormal urination

_____ Abnormal water consumption
_____ Genital discharge
_____ Mammary lumps
_____ Scooting

* = abnormal

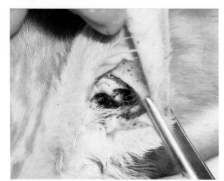

Black, waxy discharge produced by ear mites.

those structures that surround the opening into the ear. They come in a number of styles, ranging from short, pointy ones to the long, droopy variety. The external ear opening leads into the initial steep portion of the ear canal, termed the *vertical canal*, which soon bends horizontally to form the horizontal ear canal. This is where most waxy debris and moisture tends to build up, since the bend in the ear canal effectively traps it there. The ear drum, or *tympanic membrane*, lies at the end of the horizontal canal and marks the entrance into the middle ear. The inner ear, which contains the nerve endings responsible for the sense of hearing, communicates directly with this middle ear canal. Ear wax, called *cerumen*, is produced by glands lining the ear canals and forms a thin, protective barrier that maintains a constant and healthy environment within the ear. Complications arise when too much wax is produced. This can be caused by inflammation, excessive moisture and/or heat, parasites, allergies, or any other condition that threatens to disrupt the "normal environment" and pave the way toward infection. Excessive ear wax can act as an ideal growth medium for yeast and bacteria.

Signs of an ear disorder usually are easily recognized. A constant shaking of the head and scratching at the ears are sure signals that something is wrong with the one or both ears. The problem may be an infection, a foreign body (such as a blade of grass), parasites (such as ticks and ear mites), or simply an excess accumulation of hair within the ear canal. Brown to black discharges from the ears are commonly seen with ear mites or yeast infections; yellow, creamy discharges indicate that a bacterial infection is likely to be present. More serious symptoms, such as a head tilt or a circling to one side, can appear as an infection spreads into the middle ear through a diseased or ruptured ear drum. In these cases, permanent hearing damage can result if vigorous treatment is not instituted immediately.

See your veterinarian right away if you suspect an ear problem in your dog or cat. An early, proper diagnosis is essential for effective treatment, since this determines which medication is required. Needless to say, even the most minor infections can quickly become serious if not treated correctly. Furthermore, sometimes an ear disorder is merely the outward sign of a more serious disease, such as hypothyroidism or an immune deficiency. At the first sign of a problem seek help from a professional.

Now that we've seen some of the

maladies that can affect the ear, let's turn our attention to preventing ear infections. Preventive ear care is not difficult; basically, all that is involved is the use of an ear cleanser/drying agent and, if needed, a periodic ear pluck.

An ear pluck is indicated if there is visible hair occluding the opening of the ear canal. Many pet owners take it upon themselves to perform this task, but there are two reasons why this procedure should be left to a veterinarian. First, as you can well imagine, ear plucking can be a painful experience for your pet. And, as I mentioned previously, pain is a major factor that causes a pet to misbehave during a grooming session (see "A Word About Safety," page 22). As a result, this procedure has a high incidence of serious bite wounds being inflicted upon owners. The second reason for letting your veterinarian perform ear plucks is that whenever hair is forcibly removed from its follicle, inflammation occurs within that follicle. This can lead to a bad ear infection if medications are not instilled in the ears after plucking or if an actual medicated ear flush is not performed. If this is not done, you are risking doing more harm with the ear pluck than good. Suffice it to say, let your veterinarian handle this procedure.

The ears should be cleaned and dried at least twice weekly, and after bathing, swimming, or any other contact with water. Isopropyl alcohol and hydrogen peroxide can be used in combination to achieve desired

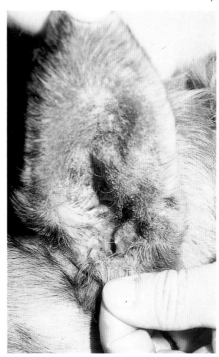

Failure to care for the ears can lead to infection.

effects, yet both can be irritating to the ear canal, especially if inflammation is present. The preferred alternative is one of the many general purpose ear cleansers available from your veterinarian or from your favorite pet supply store. Liquids are more desirable than powders, since powders can actually become storehouses for moisture once they've become saturated. Although it may seem a contradiction to apply a liquid into an area you are trying to keep dry, these preparations contain drying agents; that which remains within the ear after application will actually help create a moisture-reduced environment.

To clean the ears, first gently pull

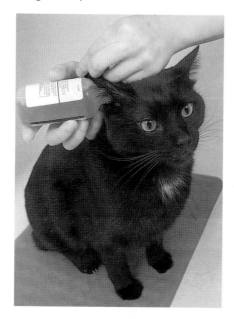

Ear cleansers help keep the ear canals dry and free from infection.

cotton ball, or cotton swab and remove any visible wax or debris from the inside of the pinna and outermost portions of the ear canal. Again, never insert anything down into the ear canal, except for the cleansing solution. If using cotton swabs, you should never lose sight of the cotton tip during the cleaning process.

One further word of caution. If your pet is showing any of the signs of ear disease mentioned above, consult your veterinarian before putting anything into the ear. If the ear drum is ruptured or has a hole in it due to its diseased nature, there is the danger of an improper medication seeping into the middle ear, causing serious complications.

the ear flap out toward you (not upwards!) to straighten the vertical ear canal. Next, instill some of the cleaning solution into each ear and massage the ears well for 15 to 20 seconds. Afterwards, release the flap and stand back: an immediate head shake should follow, and you may be surprised at what comes out of those ears! Once complete, take a tissue,

Eye Care

Eye care is a vital part of any grooming program, owing to the role that these organs play. Needless to say, special care is required to guard against inadvertent injury to the eyes when performing such grooming procedures as bathing and clipping. But just as important, pet owners must train themselves to recognize subtle (or not-so-subtle) signs that may indicate a problem involving the eyes. Inspections should be made routinely, for the sooner an abnormal condition is detected, the better the chances are for favorable treatment.

Ear swabs can be used to clean the outermost portions of the ear canal and ear flap.

The actual eyeball, or globe, is composed of many structures, all of which work in unison toward a common goal: the creation and perception of a visual image. The outer surface of the eye

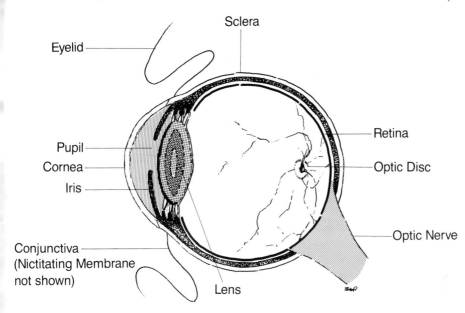

Eyelid

Sclera

Pupil

Cornea

Iris

Retina

Optic Disc

Optic Nerve

Conjunctiva
(Nictitating Membrane
not shown)

Lens

The Eye

consists of the cornea, sclera, and the conjunctival membrane. The *cornea* is the translucent structure covering the outer front portion of the globe. Composed of several layers of epithelial cells, the cornea is responsible for gathering light and directing it along the proper path to be processed. The *sclera* is that portion of the eye better known as the "white" of the eye. Though it serves no particular function as far as vision is concerned, an abnormal scleral color could mean that your pet is suffering from some underlying disease condition. Finally, the *conjunctival membrane* is a thin layer of tissue covering part of the sclera, as well as the inner portions of the eyelids. *Conjunctivitis* is a term you may have heard of; it is simply used to describe an inflammation involving this structure.

Once light passes through the clear cornea, it proceeds into the inner portions of the eye through the *pupil*, the black hole that is surrounded by the colored structure called the *iris*. As light passes through the pupil, it proceeds through the *lens*, which then focuses the image on the *retina*, located on the posterior inner surface of the eyeball. The retina, which is composed of cells and numerous tiny nerve endings, in turn transmits these messages to the brain, which ultimately translates them into the conscious perception of the image.

The eyelids of both dogs and cats function to spread the tear film secreted by the *lacrimal glands* over

Eye infections warrant prompt medical attention.

the surface of the eyes, and to protect the globes from trauma or foreign matter. Because they serve these vital needs, any disruptions or abnormalities in the normal anatomy of the eyelids, such as tumors or ingrown eyelashes, could prove disastrous to the eyes themselves if not corrected quickly.

Besides conventional eyelids, dogs and cats have third eyelids, called *nictitating membranes*, located at the inner corner of each eye. Not only are they protective in nature, they are also thought to produce some of the normal tear film. Protrusion of these structures over the surfaces of the globes may be a sign of disease, and should prompt you to seek medical attention for your pet at once.

While performing your mini-examination on your pet (see "Giving Your Pet an At-Home Physical Exam," page 33), look closely at the eyes and the lids. If you detect any abnormalities, regardless of how trivial they may seem, consult your veterinarian.

Whenever you bathe your pet, you should always apply protection to the

outer surfaces of the eyes to prevent irritation from soap. The corneas of dogs and cats are very sensitive to foreign matter and to chemicals, and may be injured easily. Even products touted as "tearless" can do significant harm if they come in contact with the corneas of dogs and cats. As mentioned previously, a sterile ophthalmic ointment is the preferred protective substance to be applied to the eyes (see "Ophthalmic Ointment or Drops," page 30). Your veterinarian should carry such ointment or, if not, can obtain it for you. When applying the ointment, be sure to keep the nozzle of the tube parallel to the eye surface. In this way, there is less chance of injuring the eye if your pet should move suddenly.

Hair that dangles in the eyes can damage the surface of the cornea and predispose to conjunctivitis and infection. As a preventive measure, be sure to trim away any hair that appears to be coming in contact with the eyes. Use only blunt-nose scissors when working around the eyes, always keeping them parallel to the edge of the eyelid.

"Tear staining" is a troublesome phenomenon seen in certain breeds of dogs, such as poodles, and even in some cats. It usually shows up as a brownish discoloration of the hair under the eyes next to the bridge of the nose. Caused by chronic inflammation and/or infection involving the tear-producing structures of the eyelids, this condition is not serious and poses no significant health hazards to those pets involved. It is, however, almost always permanent. Some veterinarians prescribe tetracycline, an antibiotic, to help reduce the amount of staining. Unfortunately, the positive results afforded by this treatment are usually only temporary. If tear-staining affects your pet there are certain measures you can take to help lessen its impact. For instance, you can wipe the affected regions on a daily basis using a dilute hydrogen peroxide (1:10) solution—being very careful to keep the solution out of the eyes. In addition, petroleum jelly applied to the corners of both eyes where the staining occurs will help divert tear flow from these regions. Many commercial products are also available to help get rid of or mask existing discoloration. As alternatives, white lipstick and zinc oxide have even been used to cover these unsightly stains. To prevent infection due to moisture buildup on the skin in the affected areas, agents used to clean and dry the ears can be used to promote dryness (see "Ear Cleansers and Drying Agents," page 29). Again, regardless of what is used, remember that you are working around the eyes. Use care to avoid the eye surfaces when applying any of these products.

Dental Care

The teeth of dogs and cats require just as much routine preventive at-home care as do the skin and coat. Only recently have veterinarians and pet owners alike concentrated on the benefits afforded by keeping the teeth

Periodontal disease can lead to secondary heart and kidney disease.

free of bacteria-ladened plaque and tartar.

Now for a brief anatomy lesson: Each tooth consists of a *crown*, that portion located above the gumline and covered by tough *enamel*; a *neck*, located at the gumline; and the *root(s)*, that portion located below the gums that is imbedded in bone. Adult dogs have a complement of 42 permanent teeth, whereas cats have 30. Aside from the total number of teeth, the anatomy and physiology (and dental care) are the same, regardless of species.

Periodontal disease is characterized by the buildup of plaque and tartar on the teeth above and below the

Professional cleaning can remove tartar deposits from under the gum line.

gum line; this in turn leads to subsequent gum inflammation and tooth loss. This affliction is one of the most prevalent health disorders affecting dogs and cats today. More than 80 percent of all dogs and cats show some indications of this disease by the time they are just three years of age. To make matters worse, dirty teeth and infected gums have also been shown to play an important role in secondary heart and kidney disease in pets.

You might ask, "But what about hard food or biscuits? Aren't these supposed to keep the teeth clean?" While it is true that the scraping action caused by chewing these hard items does help remove some tartar, the actual amounts removed are rarely satisfactory to prevent periodontal disease. In addition, in dogs and cats (as in people), these starchy foodstuffs can actually *promote* tartar buildup and bacterial growth on the teeth. As a result, using these food items as your pet's sole means of dental care may give you a false sense of security.

If dental tartar is already visible at the gum line, you will need to have your pet's teeth professionally cleaned by your veterinarian. He or she will utilize an ultrasonic dental scaler to break apart and remove the hard tartar deposits located above and below the gum line. Afterwards, the teeth will be polished to restore a smooth surface to the crowns of the teeth.

Once professional cleaning has been performed, routine at-home dental care should be started using specially formulated pet dentifrices (see "Dental Accessories," page 30). The paste or solution that you ultimately choose can be applied using a toothbrush, a soft cloth, or even your fingers. Brush as you would your own teeth. Concentrate your efforts along the gum line and outer surfaces of the teeth; if your pet will allow it, do the inside surfaces as well. Rinsing is usually unnecessary.

With respect to the frequency of brushing, daily cleaning would be ideal; at a minimum, cleanse them at least twice weekly. Many cats and dogs refuse to let their owners near their mouth. If this is the case with your pet, don't press the issue. Obviously, you don't want to get bitten in the process. All pets should receive a yearly dental checkup by your veterinarian and a professional cleaning, when needed.

Nail Care

It is very important to check your pet's nails on a regular basis to see if they need trimming. Long nails get snagged and torn easily, and also place undue stress upon the joints of

Just when you thought you've seen everything!

the paws. When a dog's paw is resting flat on the floor, the ends of the nails should not be bearing any weight. If they are, they are too long. Also remember to trim the dewclaws. Many owners whose dogs have dewclaws forget to trim the nails attached to these appendages; this can lead to ingrown toenails and infections. If present, dewclaws can be found on the inside of the front and/or hind legs, just above the paws themselves. Dewclaws serve no useful function; they represent the vestigial first digit in dogs. With few exceptions, they are usually removed by veterinarians in the first week of life, so don't be surprised if your dog doesn't have any.

Cats don't have dewclaws per se. But, unlike dogs, they do have retractable toenails that can be called into service at a moment's notice. Even though your cat may use a scratching post (or your furniture, for that matter) to sharpen those claws, they will still need periodic trimming. Feline nails tend to be more fragile than those of dogs, so use special care when clipping them.

If the nail is clear, you should be able to note the line of demarcation between the pink quick (the portion of the nail that contains the blood supply) and the rest of the nail. Using the clippers, snip off the latter portion just in front of the quick. For those pets with black or brown nails, it is slightly more difficult. Try shining a bright light (from a flashlight or penlight) on the nails before trimming to see if the demarcation can be discerned. If not,

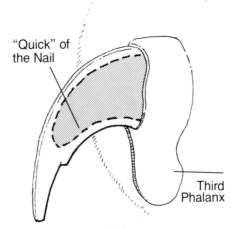

"Quick" of the Nail

Third Phalanx

The Nail

trim off small portions at a time until the nail is no longer bearing weight. On some nails, you might be able to see a little black circle in the middle of the tip. If so, start trimming the nail back, little by little. You will notice that this black ring gets bigger with each cut. When it becomes so large that it almost covers the entire end of the nail, it is time to stop.

Although you want to avoid hitting the quick, it is not the end of the world if you do so. Just apply direct pressure to the end of the bleeding nail for three to five minutes, using a tissue, cloth, or

Feline nails can shatter easily, so be sure to use a sharp pair of trimmers.

The quick is the portion of the nail containing the blood supply to the nail.

a piece of gauze. You can also use clotting powder to stop the blood flow (see "Bleeding Toenails," page 117).

Finally, many pets dislike having their feet and nails touched or manipulated. If this is the case with your cat or dog, don't press the issue. Your veterinarian or professional groomer will do it for a nominal fee.

Anal Sac Care

If you ever see your dog scooting its hind end along the floor, chances are that anal sac irritation or impaction exists. These sacs, not to be confused with anal glands, are located on either side of the anus, at about the eight o'clock and four o'clock positions. Each sac is lined with secretory cells and connects to the anus via a small duct. The fluid produced by these cells is foul smelling and can be quite irritating if allowed to remain within the sac for an appreciable amount of time. Research has shown that anal sac fluid provides a means of identification between individual animals (which explains why dogs go around "sniffing" each other). Normally, these sacs will empty every time a bowel move-

ment occurs; however, several factors can interrupt this normal emptying. For instance, obesity, inflammation (as seen with allergies), parasites, and diets low in fiber can all lead to anal sac impaction. When this occurs, the dog will resort to the scooting action mentioned above, as the dog tries to facilitate their evacuation. If the impaction is not relieved, infection can result. This disorder can also be seen in cats, but the incidence of anal sac problems in felines is quite low.

A dog's anal sac should be emptied manually only if a problem exists; this will be manifested by scooting or constant chewing or licking at the tail end. Many persons advocate emptying the anal sacs on a routine basis, whether they need emptying or not. The problem with this lies in the fact that if you go squeezing and pushing on a healthy sac, you may cause inflammation, which can subsequently lead to impaction. Thus, instead of preventing a problem, you may be creating one.

If expressing the anal sacs is indicated, there is a simple way to do it. This method involves lifting the tail with one hand and placing the thumb and index finger just below the anus at the eight o'clock and four o'clock positions, respectively. If impaction is present, you will probably feel the distended sacs under the skin. Place some tissue or cotton over the anal opening to capture the liquid. Squeeze gently, pressing inward and upward on the sacs simultaneously. This should cause the fluid contained within to be evacuated. If your first attempts do not succeed, try again. If this still doesn't release some fluid, you may need the assistance of your veterinarian. Also, let your veterinarian know if the material you obtain from the sacs is pasty, gritty, or bloody. Check for tapeworm segments (these often look like grains of rice when dry). Tapeworms are a common cause of anal sac impaction.

One last note: If you happen to get any of the anal sac material on your hands or on your pet's hair coat, wash

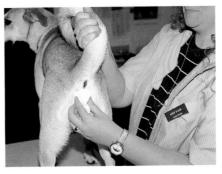

When expressing anal sacs, apply simultaneous pressure inward and upward.

first with isopropyl alcohol, then with soap and water. Since the anal sac material is alcohol soluble, water alone or even soap and water often aren't sufficient to remove this foul smell (see "Bathing and Dipping," page 47).

Brushing and Combing

Brushing helps remove dead hair and skin cells, prevents tangles and mats, spreads natural oils over the surface of the hair coat, and stimulates new hair growth. Performed daily, it will help maintain the coat in a clean and manageable condition.

Before starting a routine brushing session, spray a coat conditioner,

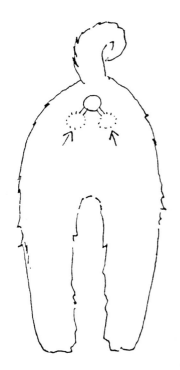

The Positioning of the Anal Sacs

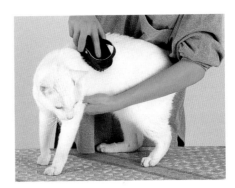

Brushing helps spread natural oils over the coat surface.

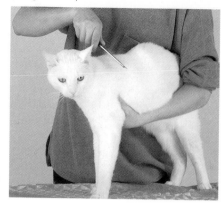

A comb can be useful in removing shed hair.

moisturizer, or even plain water onto the coat and massage it in well with your hands. This will make your brushing much easier and more effective. Once you've done this, begin brushing from head to tail, using firm but gentle strokes.

For dogs with thick hair or thick undercoats, such as the collie, chow chow, Norwegian elkhound, Pomeranian, etc., brush from the skin outward against the grain or lie to remove the dead portion of the undercoat. Use a curling motion with your brush for most effective results. Once you have covered the entire coat in this fashion, go back and brush the surface hair, this time *with* the grain.

For all other types of coats, including those of cats, brush with the grain of the hair. For long-haired cats or those dogs with thin, silky coats (such as the Yorkshire terrier), use long, gentle strokes to prevent tearing or damaging the hair. Conversely, short, wiry coats may require shorter, more vigorous strokes to achieve the desired

effects. Your pet's attitude will be a gauge of your method. If your pet is not enjoying it, you are probably being too rough in your brushing.

A comb may now be used to loosen tangles and remove any dead hair that the brush failed to get. Use it on any feathering present on the extremities, and for combing out the long hair found on the ears and face. Never use a comb on a thick undercoat, unless you are using it to help remove a mat.

For removal of shed hair that may have been missed by the brush and comb, consider using a lint brush, or even a hand-held portable vacuum—assuming, of course, that your pet will consent to its use! Finally, as an added touch, a soft cloth, glove, or velvet pad rubbed over the surface of the entire coat will help "buff" it to a nice, shiny finish.

Removing Mats and Tangles

Mats and tangles are caused by repeated chewing, licking, or scratching at a particular area on an animal's hair coat. Foreign matter such as gum can also act as a site around which a tangle, and then a mat, can develop. The most common problem areas are behind the ears, on the chest, and near the tail end, although mats and tangles can occur anywhere on the body to which the pet has access. When a mat forms, it traps dirt and moisture next to the skin and creates a perfect environment for an infection. This is compounded by the fact that the skin often becomes traumatized as the pet continues to lick and chew at the area. To avoid further problems, mats and tangles need to be removed as soon as they are noticed.

Begin by lightly moistening the mat or tangle with water or conditioner and working it free as much as possible with your fingers, comb, and/or slicker brush. If the mat is closely adhered to the skin, support its base with your fingers to prevent it from pulling on the skin. Start at the roots of the hairs and work outward. If, after much effort, you are still not successful, consider cutting out the mat or tangle with scissors or clippers. Don't worry about the lost hair; it will grow back. The main thing to remember is: *Never* try to cut out a mat unless you can clearly see where the hair meets the skin. Countless pets have been wounded by owners that failed to heed this advice. To help you achieve this line of demarcation, insert a pair of scissors or forceps into the base of the mat and then open them up, bluntly separating the matted hairs as you go. After doing this a few times, you should be able to pass a pair of scissors or clippers beneath the mat and cut it free. All this takes time and patience, not only on your part but on your pet's as well. If your pet is badly matted or particularly fractious during the procedure, it would be wise to seek the help of a professional groomer or veterinarian.

When you finally remove the mat or tangle, inspect the skin beneath to be sure it is not reddened or inflamed. If there appears to be a slight irritation, it should resolve now that the mat has been removed. If infection is pres-

A slicker brush can be used to remove tangles and mats.

Never try to cut out a mat unless you can clearly see the skin-hair junction.

ent or the area is severely inflamed, seek veterinary medical attention immediately.

Bathing and Dipping

When bath time finally arrives, the first thing you must consider is *where* the bath is to take place. For smaller dogs and cats, the bathtub, laundry tub, or kitchen sink will suffice. If your pet requires someplace larger—or if you simply refuse to share your tub—there are other options available. A garden hose and a bucket or empty milk container for rinsing will work fine outdoors. A plastic wading pool can also serve as a tub substitute. One

Brush the coat thoroughly.

Clean the ears.

Trim the nails.

word of caution: before using this, be prepared to get wet!

A number of "pre-bath" procedures need to be completed before you actually break out the water and shampoo. These can be done in or out of the tub or sink, whichever is more convenient for you:

1. Brush and/or comb the coat thoroughly.

2. Remove any tangles, mats, or unwanted hair that may be present (see "Removing Mats and Tangles," page 46). Use your clippers or scissors to remove any fecal matter that may have become matted in the hair around the tail. Trim away any hair dangling in and around the eyes using blunt-tipped scissors or clippers.

3. Swab the outer ear canal and inner ear flap gently with a tissue, cotton ball, or cotton swab to remove all visible dirt and wax, then clean both ear canals using your all-purpose ear cleanser (see "Ear Care," page 34). After cleaning, insert a cotton ball into each ear to help keep bath water from entering the canals.

4. Trim the toenails, if needed, starting with the front feet and proceeding to the hind feet (see "Nail Care," page 42).

5. Express the anal sacs, if needed (see "Anal Sac Care," page 44). It is important to do this prior to bathing rather than after, since any material or odor that contam-

inates or soils the coat will be washed away with the bath.

6. Apply ophthalmic ointment to the surfaces of both eyes for protection from soap. Keep the edge of the tube parallel to the eyelid margin (to avoid injury if your pet moves unexpectedly) and squeeze some of the ointment onto the eye surface, then manually open and close the lids to spread the ointment evenly across the cornea. If you are not sure how much to use at a time, keep in mind that it is better to use too much than too little. Be sure that the entire surface of the eye is protected (see "Eye Care," page 38).

Summary of Bathing Routine for Dogs and Cats

1. Brush and/or comb thoroughly.
2. Remove all mats and tangles.
3. Clean, swab, and pack the ears.
4. Clip the toenails.
5. Express the anal sacs (if needed).
6. Apply eye ointment.
7. Bathe and rinse.
8. Squeeze excess water from the coat.
9. Dip (if indicated) and allow the coat to air dry.
10. If no dip has been used, towel and/or blow dry.
11. After (or during) drying, brush the coat thoroughly.

Express the anal sacs, if needed.

Apply eye protection.

Apply shampoo.

Lather well.

Once you have completed these preliminary maneuvers, you are ready to bathe. If the tub or sink is being used, be sure the drain cover is in place to catch the excess hair. A piece of steel wool placed over the drain will also serve this purpose. Place a towel or, better yet, a rubber bath mat on the bottom of the tub or sink to ensure ample footing. If you do this, your pet will feel much more comfortable with this often unnerving situation. Turn on the water and let it run for a few seconds to allow the temperature to stabilize. Ideally, the bath water should be lukewarm and comfortable to the touch. If it is too cold or too hot to keep your fingers immersed in it, then it is too cold or hot for the bath.

Once the water reaches the proper temperature, lift your pet into the tub or sink and thoroughly soak the coat with water. Next, apply the shampoo. If you are applying a medicated or insecticidal shampoo, be sure to wear protective rubber gloves. Using a systematic approach, start with the neck region, then wash the back, tail end, sides, belly, underarms, and legs. Massage the shampoo into the hair and down to the skin. If needed, add water for more lather. Next, take a cloth or sponge, saturate it with water and shampoo, and carefully clean around the head and face.

Now rinse completely, using the same systematic approach that was used for the shampooing. (*Note*: If a medicated shampoo is being used, allow at least ten to 15 minutes of skin contact before rinsing it off.) Use fresh water for the rinse. It can be applied using a cup, milk jug, or hose. Double check the armpits, groin, toes, and genitalia once you are finished to be sure these areas are shampoo-free; these regions are often missed or inadequately rinsed. It is vital that all areas are thoroughly rinsed because shampoo residue that dries in contact with the skin can cause irritation and lead to chewing and other self-induced trauma.

Ideally, a conditioner should be added to the rinse water to help moisturize the skin and create a more manageable, tangle-free coat once the bath procedure is completed (see "Coat Conditioners, Moisturizers, and Emollients," page 33). Additionally, if your pet has a white coat, bluing (available at your grocery store) can be added to the rinse water to help brighten and accentuate such coats.

If the coat was especially dirty, a second shampoo and rinse may be needed. If so, repeat the above procedures step by step. Once this is complete, apply the dip if one is needed. If you plan on dipping your cat, *be sure* that the product you are using is safe for felines. Read the instructions carefully and dilute the dip according to label directions in a bucket or gallon milk jug. *For your protection, always wear rubber gloves when applying these insecticidal solutions.* Pour the dip over the neck and midline, and work it into the rest of the hair coat, using your gloves or a sponge. For the face, ears, and other hard-to-reach places, saturate a cotton ball with dip

Rinse.

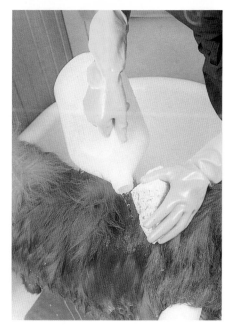

Apply an insecticidal dip, if indicated.

51

Towel drying.

Drying

If a dip is not being used, squeeze the excess water from the coat, then take a cotton towel and rub the hair briskly, starting from the head and working back toward the tail. Use a rubbing motion that is first directed with the grain or lie of the hair, then against the grain. Avoid circular motions when towel drying, as this could cause tangles and mats. Once the towel you are using becomes saturated with moisture, change to another one. Keep towel drying in this fashion until the towels no longer become saturated. To expedite the process, run a brush through the coat between towel changes. This will help prevent tangling and remove moisture. As an alternative to towels, consider using a chamois cloth, similar to the ones used to dry cars. These are very effective at capturing moisture from the coat and will make the drying quicker and easier. After towel drying, spray on a conditioner if none was previously added to the rinse water. Brush the entire coat thoroughly to work in the conditioner and undo any tangles that may have formed during the towel drying.

and apply it to these areas, always being careful to avoid the eyes. Do not rinse or towel dry after applying the dip; your pet needs to "drip dry" for best results. Feel free, however, to squeeze the excess water and dip from the coat before removing your pet from the tub or sink.

For short-coated dogs and cats, towel drying alone should suffice. Be certain to keep your pet protected from drafts or chills until the coat is completely dry. Towel drying is also the method of choice if your pet has sensitive skin or suffers from a skin ailment, since blow drying and fluff drying can aggravate these conditions. Also, some dogs and cats simply will not

Fluff drying using a blow dryer.

tolerate turning on a dryer in their presence. If this is the case with your pet, continue with towel drying. Remember, however, when using a towel as the sole means of drying you must keep your pet inside until *completely* dry. If you don't, it may search out the first patch of grass or dirt (or no telling whatever else) available and roll in it. Needless to say, you may find yourself back at the bathtub sooner than expected!

If your pet has longer hair or a thick undercoat, you may want to blow dry (fluff dry) in addition to the towel drying. All you need for this is an inexpensive hand-held hair dryer and a brush. The technique is basically the same as that used when you blow dry your own hair. With the dryer setting on warm, not hot, direct the air flow on one section of the coat and concentrate your brushing on that particular area. Direct your brush strokes against the grain or lie of the hair. The idea is to isolate and dry the hair from inside-out, starting at the moist undercoat and working out to the outercoat. Again, start at the head region and continue back toward the tail. Move from section to section, brushing and blow drying against the grain, until the coat is dry completely. If you do not want a "fluffed" appearance to the coat, finish by going back over the outercoat with your brush, brushing *with* the grain of the hair.

An alternate method of drying that many professional groomers use is cage drying. This involves placing the wet pet in a cage and attaching a

Be sure your pet is completely dry before letting it outdoors.

dryer to the cage door, effectively freeing the hands of the groomer to do other things. Under proper supervision, this is an effective and effortless way to dry dogs and cats. Unfortunately, it is also an unpractical method for the home pet groomer to use. If this method is to be carried out properly and safely, you must purchase a special dryer and a cage large enough to allow for adequate air circulation and ventilation. Just in case you were thinking about improvising, travel kennels or similar carriers *are not* ade-

Using a cage dryer.

Though oftentimes more challenging...

are willing to monitor the process closely, rely on blow drying.

Tips for Bathing Cats

Giving a cat a bath can be a very tricky procedure, to say the least. If you own one of those rare cats that doesn't mind, or even actually enjoys the water and shampoo, consider yourself lucky. More often than not, it is the cat owner who actually gets the bath—with a few claw and tooth marks thrown in for good measure. If you fall into this category, consider these tips when the dreaded bath time arrives.

Fill the tub with water and turn off the faucet *before* putting your cat in the tub. A running faucet or hose only serves to terrify your cat, so try your best to avoid using these during the bath. Use the existing water in the tub, which should come up no higher than the elbows, to wet the hair for the shampoo. Plan ahead of time and have containers filled with clean water ready for the rinse that follows. Rinse a few times, drain the tub of the dirty bath water, then rinse some more. If you have to use the faucet while your cat is in the tub, turn it on only briefly. You'll find that this will do wonders for your pet's (and your) nerves!

Most cats feel more comfortable if they have something to hold on to while getting bathed. Unfortunately, this is usually the owner's arm. A better alternative would be to place an old window screen or air conditioner filter in the tub to provide a surface to cling to. Oftentimes, cats will hold firm to

quate for cage drying. These enclosures are not designed for this purpose and do not provide adequate ventilation to be used safely. Also, although cage drying is a less labor-intensive method, it is not necessarily any faster than blow drying. In fact, it may actually take longer. For safety's sake, the air temperature from a cage dryer should never exceed room temperature because even warm air circulating within an enclosed space (especially stainless steel cages) can cause heat stress in a wet, and often nervous, pet. Compound this with poor supervision and monitoring and you have got a dangerous situation. Therefore, unless you already own the proper equipment for cage drying and this, not budging a muscle, throughout the entire bath.

Try bathing in a different location each time. Cats tend to associate locations with bad (or good) experiences. Consequently, if bath time was a bit stressful last time, you may find that the mere sight of the same tub and location will turn the bathing process into a rodeo the next time. Sometimes simply using another tub or sink rather than the one you used last time can defuse a potentially volatile situation.

the steps involved in bathing cats are essentially the same as those for dogs.

Sometimes a cat simply refuses take a bath regardless of what special steps you've taken. In this case, sedation may be required. If so, let your veterinarian perform the bath to insure the safety and well-being of both you and your pet. Never let anyone besides a licensed veterinarian administer a sedative or tranquilizer to your pet. If you do, it could be disastrous!

Dry Baths

Although not nearly as effective as wet baths, dry baths are indicated in those instances when a pet is ill or recovering from an illness and you wish to keep stress to a minimum. Dry baths are also useful for puppies and kittens less than eight weeks of age, and for pregnant dogs and cats. Corn starch and baby powder both have been used with varying degrees of effectiveness, yet with the same degree of messiness. Your best bet is to purchase one of the many commercial dry shampoos and mousses available for this purpose from your pet health care professional.

Tips for Removing Foreign Matter and Odors

If you encounter tar, paint, gum, or other foreign matter stuck to the hair, there is no need to fret. Most of these substances can . be cosmetically trimmed off with scissors or clippers in a matter of seconds. If this cannot be done without dire consequences for the coat's appearance, or if the substance is in close proximity to the skin, the following guidelines should aid in removal.

Burrs Moisten and soften the affected area with mineral oil, then comb out.

Tar Soak the affected area with mineral oil or vegetable oil and allow the oil to remain for one to two hours. Shampoo thoroughly. Be sure to rinse off well because these substances can irritate the skin. Repeat as needed. Nail polish remover will also work, but you must be careful to avoid contact with the skin.

Oil and Grease Apply plain soap or spot-treat with a waterless mechanic's hand cleaner to dissolve the grease and oil. Shampoo and rinse thoroughly. Repeat as needed.

Paint Spot-treat with turpentine or paint thinner, being careful to avoid contact with the skin. Shampoo and rinse thoroughly. Repeat as needed.

Gum Apply nail polish remover *or* a piece of ice to the gum to first harden it, then remove it with scissors, forceps, or your fingers.

Skunk Odor For those pets that have come face to face with a skunk, bathing in tomato juice, milk, or using a rinse consisting of diluted household ammonia (2 teaspoons per gallon of water) should mask and remove the smell. Skunk odor removers are also available from veterinarians and pet shops and are certainly less messy in their application. Don't become discouraged: three or more bathings may be needed before the odor is eliminated completely.

Anal Sac Odor As mentioned previously, isopropyl alcohol followed by soap and water will usually rid the coat of the secretions and odor (see "Anal Sac Care," page 44).

Chapter 5
Advanced Cosmetic Grooming Techniques

This chapter will be of special interest to those pet owners interested in the cosmetic grooming of their pets. Clipping and scissoring techniques are described, with emphasis on those cuts most commonly performed by professional groomers. The clips covered here are designed for pets, not show dogs. In addition, these cosmetic grooming techniques are useful for sprucing up an already existing haircut or style, not as a substitute for periodic professional grooming. Following the patterns and lines established by a professional groomer is much easier (and much more aesthetically pleasing) than trying to establish these yourself on your pet's coat. Don't be afraid to ask your groomer if you can watch while your pet is being groomed. Not only will this give you a chance to have your questions answered, but you will also be able to see firsthand the proper way to hold and use grooming instruments. For further information on cosmetic grooming and on particular clips not covered here, consult one of the grooming books that professional groomers use. Most of these are available at your favorite bookstore or at the local library.

Before you can achieve the desired results from at-home cosmetic grooming, you will need to invest in some additional equipment and acquire some special skills above and beyond those needed for basic home grooming purposes. A good set of clippers (such as Oster Model A5) and a variety of clipper blades are a must; thinning shears and a pair of curved scissors would also be helpful. You will need to learn the fundamentals of cosmetic clipping and familiarize yourself with the terms *scissoring*, *thinning*, *plucking*, and *stripping*. This will be the focus of this chapter.

In the next chapter cosmetic grooming techniques for some of the more popular breeds of dogs will be presented.

Clipping

To an uninitiated pet, the sound of a set of clippers can be quite unnerving. To help alleviate the tension, turn the

When using clippers, try to keep the blades parallel to the cutting surface.

clippers on and allow your pet to become accustomed to the noise before actually employing them. Hold the apparatus as you would a pencil, balancing it so that its weight is evenly distributed on both sides. This will allow you to maneuver the clippers with more agility. Keep in mind that the higher the blade number, the closer the cut.

When using, keep the blades parallel to and flat on top of the surface you are cutting. Follow the lie of the hair as if it were a roadmap, using smooth, gentle strokes. Whenever you note the hair growth changing direction, compensate with a semicircular stroke. Never force the blade through the hair faster than it can cut it. This not only will damage the blade but will also lead to clipper burns (see "Clipper Burns," page 118). Let the clipper set the pace as it cuts. Finally, always have a can of clipper lubricant spray on hand. This should be sprayed directly onto the blades during a clipping procedure whenever the blades become warm to prevent an inadvertent burning of the skin. The spray will

also keep the blades well lubricated and will help to maintain their cutting efficiency. Products such as this clipper lubricant can be purchased at most stores that carry grooming products. For added protection, also consider purchasing a clipper disinfectant spray to prevent the spread of disease during and after clipper use (see the discussion of clipper care on page 28).

Scissoring

The term *scissoring* applies to the use of scissors to "round off" rough edges of the hair coat after clipping and to remove hair from those places inaccessible or inappropriate for clippers. Scissoring is undoubtedly the hardest part of cosmetic grooming. It requires patience and practice. Control is important, not only from the standpoint of results, but also in regards to safety. To help achieve this control, be sure to grip the scissors properly. Place your thumb in the large hole of the scissors, and your ring finger (not your middle finger) in the smaller hole. Then, rest your little finger of the scissor's finger rest (if present). This hand placement will afford you the mobility to do the job correctly. When scissoring, always use a smooth, steady motion and avoid "thrusting" the scissors at the hair. When working around the eyes, keep the blades parallel to the eyelids in order to avoid injury should your pet fidget.

Before scissoring can begin, your pet must be willing to stay completely calm and still during the procedure. If this is not the case, the use of the scissors should be abandoned. Otherwise, the danger of injury is too great (see "A Word About Safety," page 22).

Thinning

Thinning is a procedure that employs thinning shears to blend different portions of the coat together and remove excess telogen hairs from the coat (see "The Hair Coat," page 14). When using thinning shears, always thin with the grain or lie of the hair, never against, for if it is done against the grain more hairs may be pulled out than desired, leaving patchy "holes" in the coat.

Plucking and Stripping

These two procedures are usually limited to terriers and other wiry-coated breeds being groomed for show. Both involve the manual removal of the actual hair from its follicle while it is in telogen, or the shedding phase of the hair cycle. By removing this dead hair prematurely, a new, fresh coat can be achieved more quickly. It is also stated that a truer, richer hair color and the desired rough texture of the coat are achieved by employing this technique.

Stripping utilizes a tool called a stripping knife to remove the hair, whereas plucking is done with the fingers. Because it is often difficult to differentiate those hairs in the telogen

Scissoring is used to smooth rough edges and "round-off" the coat.

stage from those in other stages, plucking or stripping can be quite uncomfortable for the pet. As a result, many groomers opt to use the brush and clippers in place of these techniques. Proper restraint is warranted if your pet is not accustomed to the plucking or stripping process.

When plucking, use the thumb and forefinger to grasp a small amount of hair. Pull downward sharply and quickly to remove the telogen hairs. Repeat this process over those desired portions of the coat.

If using a stripping blade, grasp the tool with four fingers, then use the thumb to press a small patch of hair against the blade. Jerk the blade in the direction of the hair growth, effectively removing the patch of hair. Continue, doing small portions at a time.

Choosing a Groomer

At one time or another, you may decide to utilize the services of a professional groomer. With so many to choose from, selecting the right groomer can be difficult. There are, however, ways to narrow the choices.

Probably the most reliable way to find a good groomer is by word of mouth. Ask your friends and neighbors who they use. If the same name keeps popping up, that is probably the one to try. If you fail to get any leads this way, consult the phone book and newspaper. Consider choosing a groomer that is close to (or in some cases, part of) your veterinarian's office or local boarding kennel just in case a problem arises during the grooming session.

Regardless of how you locate your groomer, take the time to actually talk to him or her in person before making a final decision. Does this groomer seem genuinely caring toward animals? Are the facilities clean? Does the groomer have pictures or a portfolio of his or her work? What is the protocol in case of a grooming injury or an emergency?

There are various organizations that set standards of quality and guidelines for the grooming profession as a whole. One is the International Professional Groomers, Inc. (IPG). Professional groomers certified by the IPG can be found throughout the United States and other countries, including Canada and England. Grooming skills and expertise, as well as ethical behavior, are just a few of the criteria that govern certification by this group. Other groups, such as the Professional Pet Groomers Certification Program and the National Dog Groomers Association of America, publish similar guidelines designed to assure quality within the industry. For information pertaining to certified pet groomers in your area, contact one of the organizations listed on page 128.

Once you've finally decided, take your pet over to personally meet his/her new groomer. Don't just drop your pet off and leave; be sure to hang around for the first few minutes of interaction between the groomer and your pet. This will make your four-legged friend feel more at ease.

Before you depart, be sure to leave a number you can be reached at and the number and name of your veterinarian. That way, if your pet becomes overly upset or if an accident happens, both you and your veterinarian can be contacted right away. Note: Beware of the groomer who tries to diagnose and/or treat ailments or injuries without consulting a veterinarian. Not only is this unethical and illegal behavior, but it is also endangering your pet's health as well. The same is true for tranquilization. As mentioned previously, this is only to be performed by a licensed veterinarian.

Chapter 6
Cosmetic Grooming of Some Breeds

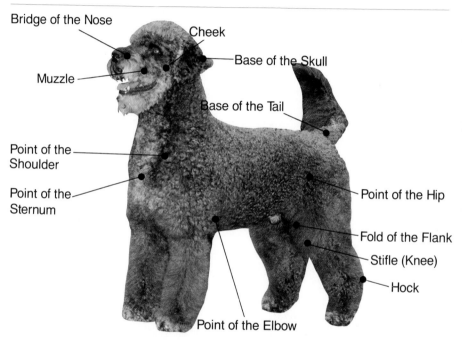

Bridge of the Nose

Cheek

Base of the Skull

Muzzle

Base of the Tail

Point of the Shoulder

Point of the Sternum

Point of the Hip

Fold of the Flank

Stifle (Knee)

Hock

Point of the Elbow

Anatomic Locations

Cocker Spaniels

The cosmetic grooming procedures in this section apply only to pet cocker spaniels. Show dogs are groomed differently.

Recommended equipment: a brush and comb, Oster A5 clippers with a #10 and #7F blade, scissors, and thinning shears. Cosmetic grooming should be performed on your Cocker Spaniel every three to five weeks.

Before starting, brush your dog thoroughly to remove any mats and tangles (see "Removing Mats and

Tangles," page 46). Then bathe and fluff dry.

Head: Using the #10 blade, clip from just behind the eyebrow region back to the base of the skull. Leave a small "dome" above the eyebrows. Clip the muzzle, cheeks, and lower jaw, directing your motion against the grain of the hair. Clip the throat area in a "V" shape, from the angles of the lower jaw to the top of the sternum.

Ears: Using a #10 blade, clip the top third of the ear both inside and out. Carefully scissor the outside edges of the clipped portion of the ear until all fuzzy hairs are removed.

Abdomen: Holding your dog up on its hind legs, clip the belly region from the navel to a point just in front of the genital area using a #10 blade. Be careful to avoid cutting the folds of skin located in the dog's flanks.

Body: Using a #7F blade, clip from the base of the skull and proceed down the back until you reach the base of the tail. Always follow the grain or lie of the hair. Then, starting at the shoulders, proceed again back toward the tail, but this time use a downward motion with your clippers on each side of the body to effectively "blend" the cut portion with the rest of the long coat. Perform this blending all the way to the base of the tail.

Tail: This area is clipped using a #7F blade. Start at the base of the tail and trim toward the end, following the lie of the hair.

The Cocker Spaniel

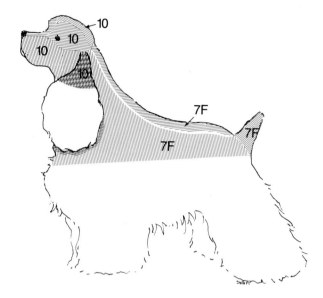

Blade Selection (side view)

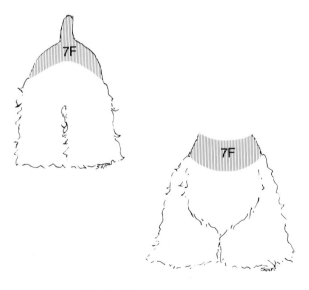

Blade Selection (rear view)

Blending: Using the thinning shears, thin the hair at the clipped-unclipped junction of the coat. This blending of the two lengths of the hair will make the pattern you just performed look more natural.

Feet: Scissor between the pads of the four paws, removing all excess hair. Then, scissor around the perimeter of the feet, making the cut edges of the hair even with the table surface.

Schnauzers

Recommended equipment: a brush and comb, Oster A5 clippers with #10 and #9 blades, scissors, and thinning shears. Cosmetic grooming should be performed on your Schnauzer every four to six weeks.

Before starting, brush your dog thoroughly to remove any mats and tangles (see "Removing Mats and Tangles," page 46). Then bathe and fluff dry.

Clipping

Head: Using the eyebrows and the corners of the mouth as markers, use a #10 blade to clip the head and lower jaw, starting from a point just behind your markers and extending to just behind the base of the ears. When clipping, use parallel horizontal strokes, following the lie of the hair. Do not clip any of the hair on the muzzle.

Ears: A #10 blade is used for the ears. Since the ear flaps are too soft to stand up against the weight of the clippers, each one must be supported firmly with your free hand. Follow the grain of the hair out from the center of the ear to the edges.

Abdomen: Holding your dog up on its hind legs, clip the belly region from the navel to a point just in front of the genital area using a #10 blade. Be careful to avoid cutting the folds of skin located in the dog's flanks.

Body: Using a #9 blade, clip from the base of the skull and proceed down the back until you reach the base of the tail. Always follow the grain or lie of the hair. Continue clipping the body down to an imaginary parallel line running from a point just above the elbows on the front legs and extending back through the top portions of the flank folds and on back to the hind end. The hind legs are then clipped on a diagonal line from the folds of the flank to a point just above the hocks, leaving fringes of hair on the front third of the legs. The front legs are left unclipped. Finally, the front portion of the neck and chest are clipped starting at the neck-head junction and ending at the sternum.

Tail: Using a #9 blade, clip the top, sides, and bottom of the tail, trimming to a slight taper at the end. Use caution to avoid the anus when clipping beneath the tail.

Once the clipping is complete, the final touch is applied by careful scissoring.

Scissoring

Feet: Scissor between the pads of all four paws, removing all excess hair. Then, scissor around the perimeter of the feet, making the cut edges of the

The Schnauzer

hair even with the table surface. The toenails should not be exposed.

Legs: Holding the scissors with the ends facing upward, trim the legs in a circular fashion, making them cylindrical in appearance. The back legs should be scissored in a similar fashion. Use your scissors or thinning shears to blend the hair at the junctions between the clipped and the unclipped portions of the hair coat.

Chest: Scissor the hair in this region from the point of the sternum to the flank region.

Eyebrows: Schnauzers have long, parted eyebrows, so begin by scissoring the hair between the eyes. Combing the eyebrows forward, scissor the eyebrow hair into an inverted "V" shape. Start at the highest point of the

eyebrows and trim at a 45 degree angle in the direction of the top corner of the ear on the opposite side of the head.

Ears: Scissor the outside edges slowly and carefully until the fuzzy hairs are removed.

Muzzle: Comb the hair on the muzzle forward. Then, using your scissors and thinning shears, remove any uneven or excessively long hairs.

Poodles

As you may know, there are many ways to clip a poodle. Described below is the Kennel Clip, one of the most popular and easy clips for pet poodles. Ideally, cosmetic grooming

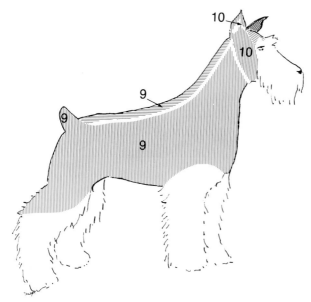

Blade Selection (side view)

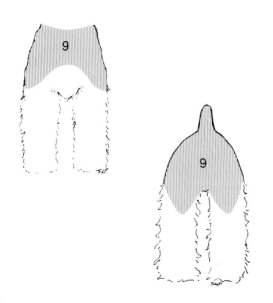

Blade Selection (rear view)

The Poodle

should be performed on poodles every three to five weeks.

Recommended equipment: a brush and comb, Oster A5 clippers with #10, #15, and #4F blades, and scissors.

Before starting, brush thoroughly to remove any mats and tangles (see "Removing Mats and Tangles," page 46). Then bathe and fluff dry.

Preliminary Procedures

There are a number of preliminary procedures that must be carried out regardless of the type of clip you maintain on your poodle.

Feet: The poodle is the only breed of dog that has its feet shaved. A #15 blade can be used to accomplish this task. Clip the front and sides of the foot, starting from the toenails and proceeding back behind the large pad of the foot. Now clip between the toes and pads using a side-to-side motion, being careful not to cut any skin webbing.

Head and Face: Use a #10 blade when clipping the face on light-colored dogs, and a #15 on dark-colored dogs. Keep the clipper flat against the skin surface to avoid clipper abrasions. Clip from the corner of the eye to the ear on both sides of the head, following a horizontal line. This first clip sets the boundaries for the topknot. Aiming the clippers at a 45 degree angle, clip the muzzle from the inside corners of the eyes to the end of the nose. Clip the bridge of the nose, starting near the eyes and working toward the end.

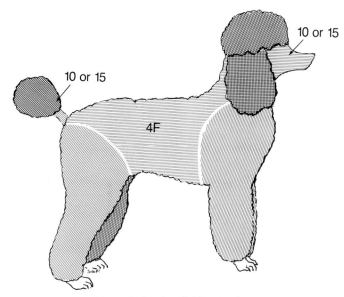

10 or 15

10 or 15

4F

Blade Selection (side view)

Holding the dog's muzzle up in the air, clip from where the neck and head meet to the end of the lower jaw.

Mustaches: Many poodle owners like mustaches on their pet's muzzle. If desired, simply omit clipping the hair on the muzzle anywhere from a point starting at the corners of the mouth and extending forward to the tip of the nose. Shape the mustache in any form or fashion you desire by using scissors.

Tail: The tail of the poodle can vary in appearance, depending on owner preference, so there is really no set way to clip it. To achieve the pom-pom look, clip the hair off the front third of the tail only. Keep the blade flat, and avoid the anal region.

Topknot, Tail, and Ears: Scissor all of these areas to achieve a rounded effect. The first cut should be made in a straight line parallel to the top of the head. Then continue trimming around the head, being careful not to cut the hair too flat or too short for your taste. The tail is done in essentially the same manner, trying to create a rounded appearance. Comb out the hair on the ears and scissor off any excessively long, uneven hairs.

Abdomen: Holding your dog up on its hind legs, clip the belly region from the navel to a point just in front of the genital area using a #10 blade. Be careful to avoid cutting the folds of skin located in the dog's flanks.

Kennel Clip

Body: Use a #4F blade for this clip. Start at the base of the neck and clip

The Scottish Terrier

straight down the back toward the tail. Be sure to stay above the level of the shoulders and hips when doing this. Next, avoiding the hair on the legs from the shoulders and hips on down toward the feet, clip the entire body between the elbows and folds of the flank, following the grain of the hair. After clipping, brush the clipped hair upward against the grain and scissor any uneven hair. Do the same for the unclipped hair on the legs to achieve a rounded appearance. Neatly trim the base of the legs where the hair meets the shaved feet.

Scottish Terriers

Recommended equipment: a brush and comb, Oster A5 clippers with #10 and #7F blades, scissors, and thinning shears. Cosmetic groom-ing should be performed on your Scot-tie every four to six weeks.

Before starting, brush thoroughly to remove mats and tangles (see page 46). Then bathe and towel or fluff dry.

Clipping

Head: Using the eyebrows and the corners of the mouth as markers, use a #10 blade to clip the head and lower jaw, starting from a point just behind your markers and extending to just behind the base of the ears. Do not clip any of the hair on the muzzle. When clipping, use parallel horizontal strokes, following the lie of the hair.

Ears: A #10 blade is also used for the ears. Only the top half of the ear is to be clipped, leaving a tuft of hair at the base and front inside edge of each ear. Follow the grain of the hair from the center of the ear to the edges.

Blade Selection (side view)

Abdomen: Holding your dog up on its hind legs, clip the belly region from the navel to a point just in front of the genital area using a #10 blade. Be careful to avoid cutting the folds of skin located in the dog's flanks.

Body: Using a #7F blade, start at the base of the skull and proceed down the back until you reach the base of the tail. Always follow the grain or lie of the hair. Continue clipping the body surface down to an imaginary parallel line running from the front point of the sternum back to the genital region. Everything below this line will remain unclipped. Finally, the front portion of the neck and chest are clipped starting at the neck-head junction and ending at the top of the sternum.

Tail: Using a #7F blade, clip the entire top portion of the tail.

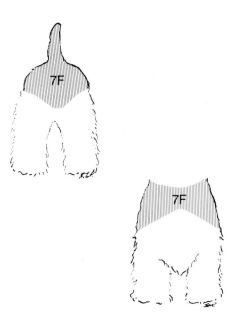

Blade Selection (rear view)

Scissoring

Feet: Scissor between the pads of the four paws, removing all excess hair. Then, scissor around the perimeter of the feet, making the cut edges of the hair even with the table surface. The toenails should not be exposed.

Legs: Holding the scissors with the ends facing upward, trim the legs in a circular fashion, making them cylindrical in appearance. Scissor the back legs in a similar fashion.

Body: Scissor the hair on the unclipped portion of the body. Next, use scissors or thinning shears to blend the hair at the junctions between the clipped and the unclipped portions of the hair coat.

Chest: Scissor the hair in this region from the point of the sternum to the flank.

Eyebrows: Scotties have long, parted eyebrows, so begin by scissoring the hair between the eyes. Combing the eyebrows forward, scissor the eyebrow hair into an inverted "V" shape. Start at the highest point of the eyebrows and trim at a 45 degree angle in the direction of the top corner of the ear on the opposite side of the head. The hair on the inner portion of the brow should remain longer than that on the outer portion.

Ears: Scissor the outside edges slowly and carefully until all fuzzy hairs are removed.

Muzzle: Comb the hair on the muzzle forward. Then, using your scissors and thinning shears, remove any uneven or excessively long hairs. Shape as desired.

Wire-Haired Fox and Welsh Terriers

Recommended equipment: a brush and comb, Oster A5 clippers with #10 and #8½ blades, scissors, and thinning shears. Cosmetic grooming should be performed on these terriers every four to six weeks.

Before starting, brush thoroughly to remove any mats and tangles (see "Removing Mats and Tangles," page 46). Then bathe and towel or fluff dry. Plucking or stripping is optional.

Clipping

Head: Using the eyebrows and the corners of the mouth as markers, use a #8½ blade to clip the head and lower jaw, starting from a point just behind your markers and extending to just behind the base of the ears. Do not clip any of the hair on the muzzle. When clipping, use parallel horizontal strokes, following the lie of the hair.

Ears: Using a #8½ blade, clip the entire outer surfaces of the ears. Follow the grain of the hair from the base of the ear to the edges.

Abdomen: Holding your dog up on its hind legs, clip the belly region from the navel to a point just in front of the genital area using a #10 blade. Be careful to avoid cutting the folds of skin located in the dog's flanks.

Body: Using a #8½ blade, start at the base of the skull and proceed down the back until you reach the

Wire-Haired Fox and Welsh Terriers

base of the tail. Always follow the grain or lie of the hair. Continue clipping the body down to an imaginary parallel line running from a point just above the elbows on the front legs through the top portions of the flank folds and on back to the hind end. The hind legs and front legs are left unclipped. Finally, the front portion of the neck and chest are clipped starting at the neck-head junction and ending at the top of the sternum.

Tail: Using a #8½ blade, clip the top, sides, and bottom of the tail, trimming to slight taper at the end. Use caution to avoid the anus when clipping beneath the tail.

Scissoring

Feet: Scissor between the pads of the four paws, removing all excess hair. Then, scissor around the perimeter of the feet, making the cut edges of the hair even with the table surface. The toenails should not be exposed.

Legs: Holding the scissors with the ends facing upward, trim the legs in a circular fashion, making them cylindrical in appearance. The back legs should be scissored in a similar fashion. Next, use scissors or thinning shears to blend the hair at the junctions between the clipped and the unclipped portions of the hair coat.

Chest: Scissor the hair in this

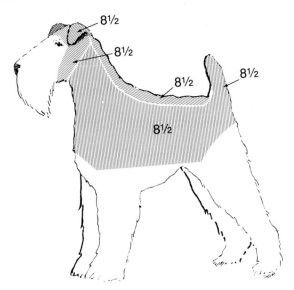

Blade Selection (side view)

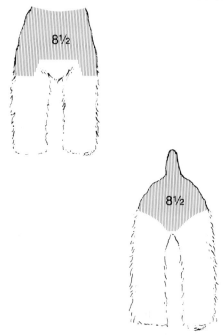

Blade Selections (rear view)

region from the point of the sternum to the flank.

Eyebrows: These particular terriers have short, parted eyebrows. Begin by scissoring the hair between the eyes. Combing the eyebrows forward, scissor the eyebrow hair into an inverted "V" shape. Start at the highest point of the eyebrows and trim at a 45 degree angle in the direction of the top corner of the ear on the opposite side of the head. The hair on the inner portion of the brow should remain slightly longer than that on the outer portion.

Ears: Scissor the outside edges slowly and carefully until all fuzzy hairs are removed.

Muzzle: Comb the hair on the muzzle forward. Then, using your scissors and thinning shears, remove any uneven or excessively long hairs. Shape as desired.

Shih Tzu

Selected Parted-Coat Breeds

The Shih Tzu, Yorkshire Terrier, Maltese, and Lhasa Apso all have one thing in common: they all have long coats parted down the middle. They are all groomed alike in regard to the body styles; the heads will differ for each breed. The Shih Tzu, Yorkshire Terrier, and Maltese all have topknots tied in bows. The Shih Tzu and Yorkie use one bow; the Maltese uses two. All four of these breeds should be groomed every 2 to 3 weeks to keep their hair coats in excellent condition.

Recommended equipment: a pin brush or natural bristle brush, soft slicker brush, comb, scissors, Oster A5 clipper with a #10 blade, bows, and small rubber bands. If a short clip is desired on these breeds, a #4 blade should be used for this purpose.

Brush-Out: The brush-out is the most important part of grooming a parted breed. Long, fine, silky coats should always be moistened with water or conditioner while being brushed to prevent static electricity, which can damage the hair. Do not saturate the coat; just spray on a fine mist. Start brushing the feet using a pin brush, or a soft slicker brush if the dog is matted. Lifting the outer coat, mist the hair with conditioner and brush from the skin outward, a few hairs at a time. Use a comb only to check for tangles. Layer brush the entire coat in this manner. Then bathe and fluff dry the dog.

Finishing: Use scissors to trim excess hair from around and between the paw pads. Then, if necessary, round off the outside edges of the feet using the table as your guide. Using your comb, part the hair down the center of the back, starting at the top of the head and moving toward the base of the tail. Once done, comb the hair straight down on both sides.

Shih Tzu

Topknot: To form the Shih Tzu topknot, part the hair from the outside corner of the eye to the corner of the ear. Grasp the hair evenly with one hand and with the other wrap a rubber band around the topknot. Place a bow at the base of the topknot.

Yorkshire Terriers

Ears: Clip the top third of the ears and scissor the outside edges smooth.

Topknot: With the hair already parted down the center of the head, part the hair again from the outside corner of the eye to inside top corner of the ear. Then, part the hair across the head from ear to ear. Grasp the hair evenly with one hand and with the other wrap a small rubber band around the topknot. Place a bow at the base of the topknot.

Maltese

Topknot: The Maltese topknot is tied with two bows. Gather the hair by parting from the corner of the eye

back to the inside corner of the ear on either side, and then across the top of the head from ear to ear. Grasp the topknot and use a comb to divide it into two portions. Each portion or side should then be doubled over and secured with a rubber band.

Lhasa Apsos

Topknot: Lhasas are usually shown without a topknot, with their hair parted down the middle the natural way. However, if a pet owner so chooses, a topknot similar to those used for the other parted breeds can be used.

Mixed Breeds

All the various styles of clips and cuts can be used on mixed breeds, depending upon what appeals to the owners. If you know the genetic recipe that went into making your particular pet, you may want to use the breed cuts of the parents. Coarse-haired dogs look the best in terrier-type clips. Poodle-type clips can also be used on a variety of mixed breeds, yet you may not want to shave the feet of these dogs, since many have large feet. Good-looking short clips, which are easy to do and care for, can be best achieved using a #4F clipper blade. Be imaginative and create the style that best suits your dog. Regardless of which clip you choose, remember that you can always change it when the dog needs to be clipped again.

Clipper Blades for Dog Grooming

Clipper Blade Size	Blade Set Cut Length (cutting against the grain of the hair)*	Comments
4F	3/8″ (9.5mm)	Excellent for body work on poodles. Creates smooth, velvety finish similar to that achieved by hand scissoring. It is also the blade of choice for short clips on the small, parted-coated breeds.
7F	1/8″ (3.2mm)	Commonly used for back work on the cocker spaniel and Scottish terrier breeds. Gives a smooth, textured look to the coat.
8 1/2	5/64″ (2.0mm)	An all-purpose blade that is ideal for terriers. Can also be used for the body work on schnauzers if a longer finish is desired.
9	1/16″ (1.6mm)	This blade gives a medium cut and a smooth finish. It leaves a textured, natural look on the body of a schnauzer.
10	1/16″ (1.6mm)	All-purpose blade commonly used for head work on cocker spaniels, poodles, schnauzers, and terriers. Can also be used for body work on schnauzers.
15	3/64″ (1.2mm)	A good, all-purpose poodle blade. Often used for trimming the feet, face, and tail of poodles.
40	1/125″ (0.1mm)	Provides surgical-grade clip to the regions to which it is applied. Can also be useful for removing mats close to the skin.

*When cutting with the grain of the hair, these lengths will approximately double.

Chapter 7

Disorders of the Skin and Hair Coat

Disorders of the skin and coat are the most prevalent types of ailments seen in pets by veterinarians across the country. Skin diseases can outnumber other medical disorders by as much as three to one, especially in areas with hot climates. If you own a pet who has never experienced such a problem, feel fortunate! Dermatopathies, the technical name for all disorders of the skin, come in many shapes and sizes, from simple flea bite dermatitis to complex metabolic and immune system diseases. In fact, there can be more than fifty different causes of hair loss alone in dogs and cats. Unfortunately, because each complaint can have a wide range of potential causes, diagnosing exactly what is going on can be difficult. Determining whether the problem is primary (occuring by itself) or secondary (occuring because of some other underlying disease condition) can be challenging as well. To give you some insight, let's see how a dermatopathy dilemma should be approached.

Diagnosis

The first factor to be considered when trying to determine the cause of a dermatopathy is its history of occurrence. Does the problem come and go with the seasons? If so, it could suggest allergies. Are any other pets (or people) in the family suffering from a similar skin disorder? If the answer is "yes," the cause could be something that is contagious to other pets and possibly to people, such as fleas, mange, or ringworm. Is the dog or cat exhibiting other symptoms of disease not seemingly related to the skin problem, such as increased water consumption, increased urination, lethargy, or weight gain? If so, the skin problem may signal some type of metabolic disturbance, such as diabetes, affecting your pet's health. Finally, have any changes been made in the household or the normal daily routine that may have precipitated the onset of the dermatopathy? Stress-related loss of hair has been known to occur in both dogs and cats in response to sudden changes in routine. A recent change in diet may indicate a food allergy. Have any new medications been given recently? Allergies to medications, called "drug eruptions," can occur, and must be ruled out as a potential cause of the dermatopathy.

Once a thorough history has been obtained and evaluated, attention should be focused on the type of pet involved. First, consider age. While all age groups can be affected, dermatopathies can be more prevalent in one age class over another. For instance, when a pet of less than one year of age is involved, parasitic, congenital (inherited), and nutritional causes of dermatopathies should come to mind. Also, though allergies may affect young and old alike, they appear much more frequently in the young to middle-aged adult dog and cat. If the pet in question happens to be older, cancer-related skin disease or metabolic disturbances such as a thyroid disorder should be considered.

Next, what breed of pet is involved? Certain breeds of dogs and cats are more predisposed to specific skin and hair coat disorders than others. For example, self-inflicted dermatitis and hair loss due to nervous licking or chewing seems to be more common in Siamese and Abyssinian cats than in other breeds. The incidence of hypothyroidism seems to be higher in Doberman pinschers and cocker spaniels than in poodles. In turn, beagles, schnauzers, poodles, and terriers have a preponderance for allergies. As you can see from these examples, apart from obtaining an adequate history, understanding breed predispositions to dermatopathies can provide valuable insight into a pet's skin condition.

Along with age and breed, the sex of your pet is also a factor to consider when evaluating disorders of the integument. For example, hypersensitivities in dogs to their own estrogen or testosterone hormones have been known to occur; itching and hair loss are the results. As might be expected in these cases, neutering provides the most effective method of treatment. Conversely, deficiencies in certain sex hormones can cause skin and coat problems as well. For example, a condition in neutered male and female cats known as feline endocrine alopecia (see "Sex Hormones," page 108) is believed to be caused by a deficiency in the sex hormones. Although these hormone-related dermatopathies are not common, they are important enough to warrant attention during any dermatopathy workup.

Look at the distribution of the skin disease or hair loss for further clues as to the origin of a skin problem. Flea allergy dermatitis in dogs almost always presents as hair loss with or without secondary skin infection along the back near the tail and along the hind legs.

Another factor to consider is symmetry. Lesions and hair loss that are symmetrical in appearance (that is, affecting similar locations on both the right and left side of the body) indicate

Relating Clinical Signs to Dermatopathies

Itching with hair loss	Skin parasites (fleas, ticks, mites, lice), allergies (inhalant, contact, flea, food, bacterial hypersensitivity, skin infections (primary or secondary), seborrhea, nutritional deficiency
Itching without hair loss	Same as above, yet in early stages
Hair loss without itching	Hormonal imbalances, ringworm, telogen effluvium, congenital (inherited), demodectic mange, nutritional deficiency, excessive licking (neurodermatitis)
Dry, flaky skin	Seborrhea, nutritional deficiency, overbathing, underbrushing
Oily, greasy skin and hair	Seborrhea, stud tail (cats), poor self-grooming, (seen especially in sick cats)
Scabby, crusty skin	Skin infection (primary or secondary), mange, bacterial allergy, seborrhea (dogs), feline miliary dermatitis (cats)
Bad odor to skin and hair coat	Seborrhea, skin infection (primary or secondary), ear infection, tooth and gum disease, anal sacs
Thickened skin with hair loss	Hygroma or Lick Granuloma, hypothyroidism, any chronic (long-term) dermatopathy
Color (pigment) changes to the skin and/or hair	Genetic, trauma to skin (physical or chemical), any chronic (long-term) dermatopathy, Acanthosis Nigricans, skin cancer, hormonal dermatopathies
Small, red bumps and/or pustules on skin surface	Allergic response, skin infection/folliculitis, parasites (such as mange mites)
Lumps and masses	Abscesses, lipomas, skin tumors, granulomas, sebaceous cysts
Raw, moist, open sores on skin	Hot spots, Lick Granuloma, Eosinophilic Granuloma (cats), solar dermatitis, skin tumor
Excessive grooming/licking	Neurodermatitis, Lick Granuloma, skin parasites, skin infection

that some sort of generalized disturbance is going on, such as a metabolic disease or an allergy. In contrast,
lesions that do not exhibit symmetry
can often be attributed to parasites,
primary skin infections, or other localized causes.

The signs involved with the dermatopathy, including appearance, should
help narrow the choices. Of all the
complaints regarding the skin and
coat of dogs and cats, itching and hair
loss lead the list.

Most pet owners would agree that it
is frustrating to have an itchy pet. The
relentless scratching and chewing,
with enough tufts of torn-out hair lying
around to knit a sweater, not only drive
your pet crazy, but can drive you
insane as well. Anything that can
cause skin inflammation can cause
itching. In dogs and cats, the two
most notable culprits are skin parasites and allergies. However, don't be
too hasty to set the blame on these.
Other disorders can cause similar
signs as well.

Hair loss is often the unhappy by-
product of relentless chewing and
scratching by the pet, and of the
inflammation affecting the hair follicles. Because itching and loss of hair
tend to go hand in hand, it is difficult to
talk about one without the other. However, realize that both do not always
have to occur together. As we will see
later, one hallmark of metabolic skin
disease in pets is hair loss without any
accompanying itching or scratching.
Similarly, the fungal infection known
as ringworm may appear as hair loss

without any noticeable scratching,
assuming the inflammation caused by
the organism is minimal. Is it possible
to see itching without loss of hair?
Indeed it is, especially in the early
stages of any skin disease. However, if
relief from the itching and inflammation is not swift, hair will soon start to
fall out.

Besides itching and hair loss, dermatopathies can assume a number of
different presentations. Some of the
more common signs and appearances observed in dog and cat skin
diseases, as well as the potential
causes for each, are listed in the table
on page 80.

As illustrated, diagnosing dermatopathies in dogs and cats can get quite
involved. Many factors need to be
taken into account. What appears to
be a clear-cut case of fleas may actually turn out to be something completely different. This is where your
veterinarian can help. Don't try to diagnose your pet's skin condition yourself! The guidelines presented here
are meant to give you some idea of
what might be occuring, but for a
definitive diagnosis, expert attention
is essential. The goal is not to obtain
a diagnosis, but to obtain a *correct*
diagnosis!

When you take your pet to your veterinarian for a dermatopathy evaluation, expect certain diagnostic tests to
be performed. The table on page 85
lists some of these helpful diagnostic
tests and the purpose for doing them.
Many times a trained eye can make a
diagnosis immediately; other times a

Humans are at risk of contacting ringworm from their pets (left). Performing a skin scraping for mange (right).

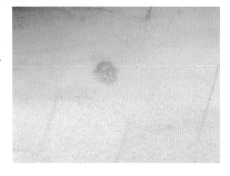

Dermatopathies involving young pets are often parasitic, nutritional, or congenital in nature.

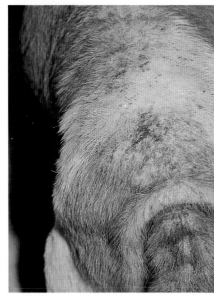

The distribution of the dermatopathy can give valuable insight as to the origin of the problem.

whole series of tests will be required to elucidate the cause of the skin disease. It is in your pet's best interest to have them done.

Treating dermatopathies can be just as difficult and involved as the diagnosis. Any treatment performed should first be directed toward the underlying diseases that may be causing the skin condition, then against the lesions involving the actual skin and coat. Traditionally, antibiotics, adrenalcortico-steroids (anti-inflammatory medications), and pesticides, used alone or in varying combinations, have been the standard treatment for almost all types of dermatopathies in dogs and cats. However, in recent years new drugs, supplements, and medications (such as those discussed in "Fatty Acids," page 18) have been developed to complement these conventional therapies and, in some instances, to replace them. This is certainly good news for those pets who are at risk from the potentially dangerous side effects of long-term steroid use. As each of the following dermatopathies are examined more closely, the treatment alternatives will be discussed further.

Skin Parasites

Fleas

Fleas are the most irritating pests encountered by pet owners. Millions of dollars are spent each year on flea-control products and services alone in a desperate attempt to provide relief to itchy dogs and cats. This control becomes even more important due the fact that dogs and cats aren't the only ones fleas will annoy. If they get hungry enough, fleas will attack people as well! In this respect, they can become a direct public health threat, since fleas are known carriers of diseases such as endemic typhus and bubonic plague. They can also act as the intermediate host for tapeworms, and can transmit these to pets and, in some cases, to people.

The life cycle of the flea requires from two weeks to two years to complete, depending on environmental conditions. Maturity occurs most rapidly when the temperature is between 65°F (18°C) and 95°F (35°C) and the relative humidity is between 50 and 99 percent (no wonder they are such a problem in warm climates!). The adult flea will lay three to 18 eggs per laying, which usually fall off the host after being laid and may be deposited directly into the environment. The white, worm-like larvae that emerge from the eggs avoid light and feed on adult flea excrement ("flea dirt") or particles of organic material in the environment. When the larvae mature nine to 200 days later, they spin a cocoon where they stay for

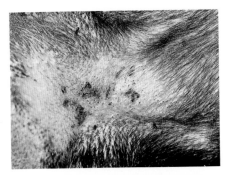

Fleas are one of the most difficult parasites to control.

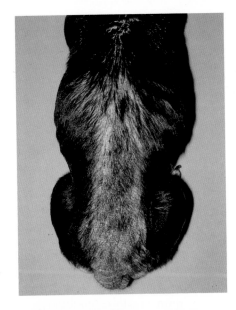

Characteristic hair loss caused by fleas.

Premise control is the most vital part of any flea control program.

seven days to a year, depending upon environmental conditions. At this stage they are very resistant to chemical or environmental treatment. Once they hatch from the cocoon, they start looking for a host to feed on, thus repeating the cycle. The average adult flea can live up to 58 days without food; however, some species, after engorging on a blood meal, can live 200 days without a fill-up!

Be aware that fleas will spend only a small portion of their time feeding on your dog and cat. The rest of the time is spent napping or laying eggs in your carpet, furniture, bedding, or yard. As a result, don't be surprised if you look but can't find an actual flea on your pet. In dogs, one sign to look for that can indicate the presence of fleas is visible chewing and hair loss around the hind legs and the back, near the base of the tail. If you part the hair (or what's left of it) in these areas, you will often see the tiny black flecks of flea excrement that are left behind after feeding. In cats, fleas tend to be more commonly found in the neck region than in the hindquarters. Because the scratching can be intense, it is not uncommon to find crusts and scabs lining the neck area of a cat infested with fleas (see "Miliary Dermatitis," page 114). As with dogs, look for the tiny black flecks—a sure sign that you and your cat are not alone!

Make no mistakes about it: Flea control is difficult! Treatment of the pet alone is insufficient, since fleas spend most of their time in the environment actually off the host animal. As a result, environmental or premise treatment is the most important part of any flea control program.

House and Yard Treatment

1. Vacuum carpets, floors, and your pet's sleeping quarters to remove dirt, eggs, and larvae. Vacuum bags should be disposed of afterward to get rid of any live fleas or flea larvae contained within. If a nondisposable bag is used, keep moth balls in the bag at all times to kill any larvae or fleas collected.

2. Have the house (and your pet's house) treated, either by hiring a professional exterminator or by spraying, dusting, or fogging yourself. Be sure to remove all pets, including birds and fish, from the premises before doing so. Spot treat furniture, baseboards, and floor cracks, since fleas tend to breed in these areas. Products containing methoprene (see the table on page 88) should be used in conjunction with standard adult-killing products in order to prevent the further development of any pre-adult fleas still in the area. Consult your veterinarian or pet health care professional for recommendations on which brands are the most effective.

3. Treat the yard for fleas with a product approved for this purpose. Concentrate on areas under shrubbery and those

Diagnostic Aids for Dermatopathies

Test	*Purpose*
Skin scraping	Detects mange mites, other parasites
DTM (Dermatophyte Test Medium)	Tests for the presence of ringworm
Woods Lamp (ultraviolet light)	Tests for the presence of ringworm
Cytology	Microscopic examination of fluid or cells from skin lesions; preliminary test for cancer
Skin biopsy	Microscopic examination of a tissue sample; definitive test for cancer and autoimmune diseases
Bacterial culture/sensitivity	Identifies types of bacteria involved in a skin infection; determines which antibiotics that particular organism is sensitive to
Blood and stool parasite checks	Detects internal parasites, some of which can cause itchy reactions
Complete blood count/serum biochemical profile	Identifies underlying internal diseases (such as diabetes, Cushing's disease, allergies, etc.)
Hormonal assay	Detects hormonally related dermatopathies
Allergy testing (skin testing or blood testing)	Helps determine what substances a pet is actually allergic to

places that your pet frequents the most (such as shady areas).

4. Repeat steps 1, 2, and 3 in two weeks to eliminate any newly hatched fleas, and again at regular two- to four-week intervals throughout your area's entire flea season.

Treatment for the Pet

At the same time that you are treating your house and yard, you need to be treating your pet. There are many different preparations available for use directly on dogs and cats, and even some designed to be taken internally. Have your veterinarian help you formulate a customized plan for flea control designed to suit your pet's individual needs, using one or more of the numerous products available for this purpose. The following is a list of such products or preparations and some comments about each.

Dusts and Sprays. These products can contain any one of a number of active ingredients that vary in terms of effectiveness, duration of action, and toxicity. Whether you choose to use a dust or a spray is entirely up to you.

One possible advantage of dusts and powders is that their application seems to be tolerated much more favorably than sprays; as far as effectiveness is concerned, there is little difference. When applying sprays to cats, small dogs, and puppies, here's a helpful hint: Spray some of the product onto a wash cloth or towel, then use this to apply the spray onto the coat. Always start at the head region and work back toward the tail. This keeps the fleas from running and hiding in tough-to-reach places around the eyes and ears.

Where cats are concerned, consider using a towel to apply a flea spray.

Flea Collars. Used in conjunction with other types of treatments, flea collars can be quite effective; alone, they rarely are sufficient. If you do choose to use a collar on your pet, don't apply it tightly. For cats that spend time outdoors and unsupervised, consider purchasing a breakaway flea collar for its added safety.

Flea Shampoos and Dips. These products have active ingredients similar to those found in dusts and sprays. Be sure to use them only as directed. Remember, dips are to be left on the pet to dry, not rinsed off or artificially dried (that is, by towel, blow dryer, etc.).

Oral and Systemic Flea Medications. These products are available from your veterinarian and should be used only under his or her close supervision. Do not use shampoos, dips, sprays, dusts, or collars in conjunction with these products unless your veterinarian advises it. In some difficult cases, systemic treatment may be the only thing that proves effective. How-

There are lots of flea and tick products to choose from.

ever, one major disadvantage of these formulations is that fleas must actually bite the pet in order to ingest the medication and die, thereby rendering these products less than desirable for those pets that are allergic to flea bites themselves.

Other less conventional methods of flea control have been used, yet for most, there is no scientific proof of their efficacy. Brewer's yeast, garlic, thiamine, and certain other vitamins have been used in an effort to prevent or kill fleas. Similarly, electronic flea collars and other electronic devices either worn by the pet or placed within the house also have many proponents. The usefulness of these devices, as well as the foodstuffs mentioned above, is highly questionable. Some people swear by them; others have the opposite opinion. I tend to agree with the latter, but I'll let you be the judge!

One word of caution: Regardless of the type used, never use any treatment on a cat unless its label states that it is approved for cats. Always read and follow label directions carefully and, for your pet's safety, avoid combining different types of treatments or chemicals without first checking with your veterinarian.

Ticks

As with fleas, ticks pose a health risk not only to your pet, but to you as well. Ticks can cause damage to their host animal just by sheer numbers, causing anemia due to loss of blood. Their saliva can also be irritating and,

Both ticks (above) and fleas (below) can carry diseases harmful to man.

Using tweezers to remove a tick.

Sarcoptes scabiei *and mite eggs.*

Common Ingredients of Flea and Tick Control Products

Active Ingredient	Comments
Pyrethrins	Derived from chrysanthemums; very safe; quick kill; poor residual activity; salivation may be seen after applying
Permethrin, Tetramethrin, Fenvalerate, d-transallethrin, Resmethrin	Synthetic pyrethroids; similar to pyrethrins, yet some may have longer residual activity, higher toxicity; salivation may be seen after application
Rotenone	Derris root extract; more toxic than pyrethrins, yet still relatively safe
d-Limonene, Linalool	Citrus peel extract; relatively safe; questionable efficacy
N-Octyl Bicycloheptene Dicarboximide, Piperonyl Butoxide	Synergists that increase the effectiveness of pyrethrins and some pyrethroids
Carbaryl, Propoxur, O-Isopropoxyphenyl Methylcarbamate	Carbamate insecticides; more potent (and toxic) than pyrethrins; good residual activity; use extreme caution when using in combination with other products containing carbamates or organophosphates; signs of toxicity include tremors, salivation, diarrhea, convulsions, constricted pupils
Chlorfenvinphos, Chlorpyrifos, Diazinon, Phosmet, Dichlorvos, Dioxathion, Malathion	Organophosphate insecticides; more potent (and toxic) than pyrethrins and many carbamates; good residual activity; use extreme caution when using in combination with other products containing carbamates or organophosphates; signs of toxicity include tremors, salivation, diarrhea, convulsions, constricted pupils.
Fenthion, Cythioate	Systemic organophosphate insecticides; should not be used in combination with other products containing carbamates or organophosphates; signs of toxicity same as those for topical organophosphates; should not be used on cats
Amitraz	Used to treat *Demodex* mange; fairly low toxicity; side effects can include transient sedation and drowsiness, which may last up to 48 hours
Methoprene	Insect growth regulator; often used in combination with other products; inhibits maturation of flea larvae

in some cases, toxic. These parasites also transmit a number of diseases to both man and animals, including Rocky Mountain Spotted Fever, Lyme Disease, and Erlichiosis. For these reasons, controlling ticks is essential.

Since ticks are sensitive to the same type of chemicals as fleas, control of these parasites on dogs and cats is basically the same procedure. A topical flea and tick spray or powder is the best thing to use to kill ticks on your pet. For efficacy's sake, forget those folk remedies, such as suffocating the tick with vaseline, gasoline, or alcohol, or applying a hot match or needle to the tick's body. Not only do they fail to work most of the time, but they can also hurt your pet and be irritating to the skin. For tick control off your pet, use a yard and premise pesticide spray. Be sure to apply it not only to the lawn, but to the surrounding trees and shrubbery as well. (Make certain the pesticide is safe to use on your particular shrubbery before applying!) And keep in mind that ticks can live for months in their surrounding habitat without a blood meal, so treat the environment every two to four weeks during the peak flea and tick seasons (spring and summer), and every eight to twelve weeks during the remaining months.

Most ticks that are on your pet will simply fall off in time once they have been killed. In some cases, though, you may need to manually remove the dead tick after spraying. When picking them off your pet, never use your bare hands because if you happen to get any of the tick's bodily fluids on you, you could be exposing yourself to disease. Use tweezers or gloves instead. Grasp the tick as close to its head as possible and pull straight up, using constant tension. Once the tick is freed, wash the bite wound with soap and water and then apply a first aid cream or ointment to prevent infection. Again, be sure the tick is completely dead before removal; this will insure that the tick's mouthparts come out attached to the rest of the body. If left behind, the mouthparts can cause irritating localized reactions or bumps that can linger for quite some time.

Mites

Mange mites are likened to "microscopic ticks" that live within the skin or hair follicles and feed on body fluid, including blood and cellular debris. They often cause a crusty dermatitis that leads to hair loss and secondary infection. In all, there are four types of mange mites that are of special significance in dogs and cats.

Sarcoptic mange, caused by *Sarcoptes scabiei*, is characterized by itching, prominent hair loss, and/or thickened, wrinkled skin, especially around a dog's face, ear tips, elbows, thighs, and tail. Notoedric mange, caused by *Notoedres cati*, is the feline counterpart of the dog sarcoptic mange mite, and has a similar distribution pattern. Both of these mange mites actually burrow into the skin of their host; this induces inflammation and causes an intense itching sensation.

Demodectic mange on the face of a Chow Chow.

Cheyletiella, or "Walking Dandruff." Note the dandruff-like flakes, which are the mites themselves, on the floor next to this dog.

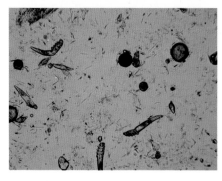

The characteristic "alligator" appearance of the Demodex mange mite.

The mange mite, *Cheyletiella* — better known as "walking dandruff"— also causes a variable amount of itching in infested dogs and cats, but, unlike sarcoptic or notoedric mange, this mite lives primarily on the surface of the skin. It gets its name from the fact that it if you look closely, the scales and dandruff produced by the infestation will appear to be moving or "walking" around, owing to the activity of the mite.

In contrast to these first three mites, the demodectic mange mite, *Demodex canis*, resides within the hair follicles of its canine host, often causing secondary folliculitis and infection. By itself, it usually doesn't cause the severe itching we see with sarcoptic mange, but if the hair follicles become infected, itching can become a significant factor. Of all the mange mite infestations, *Demodex* is probably the most serious, since it usually indicates that some type of an immune disorder or immune suppression exists in the host animal. Because of this, it is often difficult to treat and cure. Cat owners don't have to worry as much about this type of mange, since *Demodex* is rare in felines.

Your veterinarian will observe clinical signs and obtain and examine skin scrapings to diagnose mange in your dog or cat. It is essential that a proper diagnosis is made, since treatments vary between the different types of mange. Treatment for sarcoptic, notoedres, and cheyletiella mange classically consists of, among other things, organophosphate shampoos and dips (see the table on page 32). Treatment for demodectic mange requires the use of a special type of dip (amitraz) and, if secondary skin infection is present, antibiotic therapy. Other adjunctive treatments, such as vitamin E and zinc therapy, may also be employed, since *Demodex* can be difficult to treat effectively.

Sarcoptes, Notoedres, and *Cheyletiella* are all contagious to humans, although most of the time the infestation is self-limiting. However, if your pet is diagnosed with one of these types of mange, and you or someone in your family has itchy skin lesions, be sure to contact your physician immediately.

Another type of mite affects dogs and cats as well. *Otodectes cynotis,* better known as the ear mite, lives not in the skin or hair follicles, but in the external ear canals. Infestation with this mite is characterized by head shaking, scratching at the ears, and a black, crusty discharge in the ears. "Hot spots" may even appear under and around the ears due to the intense scratching. Traditionally, treatment for ear mites consists of placing a few drops of mineral oil or ear mite medication into the ears daily for a week or two to kill the mites. But many pet owners can testify that this does not always work. One major reason is that when your pet scratches at its ears, mites will often translocate to the extremities and from there will begin their long journey back to the ears via the coat. Unless you exterminate these misplaced mites, they will reinfest the ears you treated so diligently.

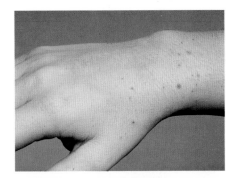

Sarcoptic mange can be transmissible to humans.

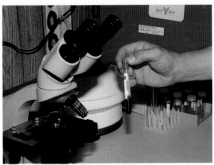

Thanks to research, testing for allergies is now an easy process.

Antihistamines (smaller capsules), coupled with special fatty acid supplements (larger capsules), have shown some promise in the treatment of inhalant allergies.

A flea collar caused this case of contact allergy.

The secret is to use a pyrethrin-type flea spray or shampoo on your pet's coat at least twice during your treatment. By treating not only the ears, but the hair coat as well, you will be assured of a thorough elimination of these pests.

Lice

Dogs and cats can become infested with lice, which, in turn, can cause itching, secondary skin infection, and hair loss. However, the importance of these parasites as far as skin disease is concerned is minimal when compared to fleas, mange mites, and ringworm. Severe infestations can be detrimental to the health of the animal, but rarely do such cases occur in dogs and cats kept and cared for as pets. Most cases of lice infestation occur in animals that are grouped together with other animals in less-than-sanitary environments. Shampoos, dips, and sprays designed to kill fleas and ticks will also prove effective against lice, and should be used weekly for three to four weeks if this particular parasite is diagnosed.

Allergies

Next to fleas, allergies receive most of the blame for the itching episodes that occur in dogs and cats. Allergic reactions are the result of overly reactive immune systems responding to the presence of foreign substances called *allergens*. The severity of these reactions vary in each individual case, yet the standard outcome is a very uncomfortable pet! We can classify allergies in dogs and cats into four main groups. These include inhalant allergies (atopy); contact allergies; flea allergies; and food allergies.

Inhalant Allergies

Inhalant allergies, better known as "atopy," can develop at any age, although 70 percent of the cases develop between one to three years of age. Oddly enough, this disease has not been documented in cats; however, there is evidence that it may exist nonetheless. Face rubbing, feet biting, and armpit scratching are the most frequent signs seen with this disorder. Small red bumps, called *papules*, may appear on the skin surface in some cases. Affected pets will often scratch and chew so much that hair loss and secondary infection results, leading to even more itching. Ear inflammation and infection may also accompany even mild allergic reactions.

Allergies to grasses, weeds, trees, and shrubs often come and go with the seasons, whereas allergies to house dust, dander, hair, and fungi may be a year-round problem. Diagnosis of atopy in pets is based on history and clinical signs, as well as allergy testing. Once diagnosed, however, treatment can be frustrating, since it is highly unlikely that you will be able to completely avoid or eliminate the offending allergen(s).

Traditionally, steroids have been used to reduce the inflammation and itching caused by inhalant allergies, but the continuous, long-term use of steroids can have serious adverse effects on your pet's health. Desensitizing allergy injections, which consist of extracts containing those substances to which the patient is actually allergic, certainly provide a safer alternative to steroids, but in some cases may not be as effective and may take longer for favorable results. However, allergy testing for pets has become much easier and more commonly practiced in recent years. Now, in addition to the old method of intradermal testing, which involves actually injecting the offending substances into the skin and watching for an allergic response, newer methods that simply test blood serum samples from allergic pets for offending agents have been developed. As a result, treating allergies using extracts based on allergy testing results is becoming more and more popular. A new type of treatment, involving the use of antihistamines coupled with special fatty acid compounds (see "Fatty Acids," page 18) has also shown some promise in treating atopy, without the side effects associated with steroid usage. Consult your veterinarian for more details.

Contact Allergies

Contact allergies occur when the skin comes in direct contact with an allergen. Plants, plastic bowls, carpets, shampoos, chemical cleaners and flea collars are all common offenders. Because of the nature of the allergy, those areas most affected include the nose, face, feet, and belly. The signs seen with contact allergies

are similar to those of inhalant allergies, and differentiation of the two can often be difficult. With contact allergies, removal of the offending agent or substance will eliminate the condition. In the case of chemicals, sprays, and other topical products, thorough rinsing with water should be performed. If the feet are involved, care must be taken to keep the affected skin dry in order to prevent an infection from becoming established. Immediate removal of offending flea collars is also indicated.

Flea Allergies

Flea allergy dermatitis is different from flea bite dermatitis in that in the latter the actual itching and irritation occurs at the actual site of the bite. In the case of a flea allergy, however, the saliva of the flea acts as the allergen and can cause an allergic response anywhere on the body. As previously indicated, lesions in dogs typically start on the back near the base of the tail and on the inner hind legs. From there, they can spread forward. In cats, miliary, or seed-like, crusts are commonly found around the head and neck. Obviously, the best way to treat such an allergy is to control the fleas on the pet and in the environment (see "Fleas," page 83), and to control any secondary skin infection.

Food Allergies

Food allergies are blamed for many itchy dogs and cats, yet in reality they account for only a small percentage of the "allergies" seen by veterinarians. Signs of a food allergy are the same

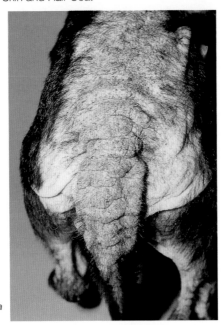

Thickened skin and hair loss caused by a flea allergy.

gen. Rations fed during these trials consist of specially formulated "hypo-allergenic" diets, usually containing-ingredients such as lamb, cottage cheese, and whole grain rice. If eventually diagnosed with such an allergic problem, your pet will need to be maintained on this special diet to prevent a recurrence of the dermatopathy.

Hives

Hives, technically known as *urticaria*, are numerous small, raised patches of skin and hair (wheals) that appear all over the body or, in some instances, are localized to one particular region. Intense itching always accompanies their formation. The presence of hives indicates that an acute allergic reaction of some sort has taken place. This sometimes occurs after an insect sting or vaccination. Since allergic reactions such as these can be serious if swelling occurs around the face and neck, veterinary advice should be sought at once. Antihistamines and/or anti-inflammatory medications are required to control these reactions.

Allergic Reactions to Drugs and Medications

Allergies to drugs have been known to occur and should be considered whenever a dermatopathy appears concurrently with the administration of a vaccine or medication, the latter either by mouth or injection. Though signs associated with these allergic reactions can be quite variable, most are characterized by intense itching.

as those seen with other allergies (that is, itching, hair loss), but with some cases gastrointestinal disturbances, such as vomiting and diarrhea, may also be present. In cats, miliary dermatitis (see "Miliary Dermatitis, page 114) may appear, marked by intense itching and scabbing around the face and head. A recent history of a change in the type or brand of food fed to a pet is often seen with food allergies. Dietary culprits can include milk or milk products, any type of meat, cereals, food additives, and even substances found in the drinking water.

Diagnosis of a food allergy can be frustrating, since it involves food trials, which are usually conducted over a time span of three to six weeks in an attempt to uncover the offending aller-

As you would expect, discontinuing the medication is the treatment of choice.

Bacterial Hypersensitivity

Bacterial hypersensitivity is somewhat like an allergy, except that it is not caused by something inhaled, eaten, or touched. Instead, it is caused by an exaggerated immune reaction to the bacteria that normally reside on the skin surface. This condition is much more prevalent in dogs than in cats, and can be made worse by the presence of any of the other allergies mentioned previously. These hypersensitivities are characterized by small pustules and/or circular patches of hair loss due to folliculitis distributed over the entire coat (see "Folliculitis," page 99). In fact, this condition can be easily mistaken for a case of ringworm if diagnostic tests are not performed. Many dogs suffering from this type of allergy also have an underlying thyroid disorder; therefore, a thyroid test should be always be included in the veterinary diagnostic evaluation. Treatment for this dermatopathy is similar to that for folliculitis: antibiotics, topical medications and shampoos, and anti-inflammatory medication. Other medications, such as thyroid hormone supplements, may be indicated as well. In especially severe cases, administering desensitizing allergy injections consisting of killed preparations of the offending bacteria

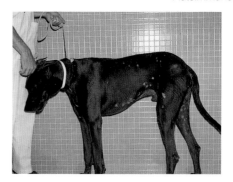

Bacterial hypersensitivity.

or parts of the same may help. Regardless of which treatments are used, this is a difficult disorder to control due to the nature of the immune system activity. Recurrences are common, and treatment may need to be provided indefinitely.

Autoimmune Skin Diseases

Autoimmune diseases, like allergies, are caused by overreactive immune systems. The difference is that with allergies, the body is allergic to some outside allergen; with autoimmune disease, the body is actually "allergic" to its own tissues, which can include the skin. If you are a cat owner, you can relax; these diseases are extremely rare in felines.

In dogs, *pemphigus* is the term used to describe a series of autoimmune diseases that affect the skin. These are characterized by reddened ulcerations and blisters that can be found anywhere on the body, especially around the mouth and lips.

These lesions are itchy and usually quite painful.

Other autoimmune diseases affecting the skin of dogs exist, but the incidence of occurrence is infrequent. Diagnosis of any such disease, including pemphigus, requires a skin biopsy and laboratory evaluation. If diagnosed, treatment most often consists of high dosages of steroids in an attempt to modulate the immune system's activity. Obviously, when using steroids in this manner, close veterinary supervision is essential.

Ringworm and Other Fungal Infections

Ringworm, known as *dermatophytosis*, is not a worm at all; it is a fungus that attacks the skin, hair, and even sometimes the nails of both dogs and cats. A circular patch of hair loss with or without secondary skin infection is the classic lesion seen with this parasitic disease. Yet keep in mind that this clinical manifestation does not occur in every case. In fact, cats and ring-

worm are so well adapted to each other that felines may not show apparent signs of infection. Thus, undetected ringworm can spread to other pets in the household, and to people as well! In addition, dogs and cats can become infected with ringworm from dirt and soil; therefore, contact with an infected animal is not always needed for transmission.

Because of its potential for causing disease in humans, ringworm must always be suspected as a cause of hair loss in dogs and cats. An examination and/or fungal culture can verify or eliminate such suspicions. Treatment of ringworm is accomplished through the use of topical antifungal medications, shampoos, and/or oral medications. Be prepared to spend some time with this condition because some cases can take six to eight weeks, sometimes longer, to be resolved.

Unfortunately, ringworm is not the only type of fungus that can affect the skin of pets. Though their occurrence is somewhat uncommon, other, more serious types of fungus can infect the skin of dogs and cats. This skin involvement is usually characterized by the formation of firm nodules (see "Lumps or Masses," page 110) or by ulcerated, draining lesions. To make matters worse, these fungi simultaneously can attack the internal organs of the host and do considerable damage if not detected early. Prompt treatment with antifungal medication is needed for satisfactory recovery in these cases.

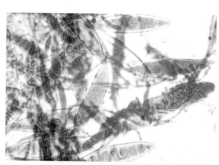

As this microscopic slide reveals, ringworm is not a worm at all; it is a fungus.

Bacterial Skin Infections

Although they can arise spontaneously in dogs and cats, bacterial skin infections are more likely to appear secondarily to another condition. For example, physical or chemical trauma (wounds and abrasions), parasitism (fleas, mange, etc.), abnormal immune response (allergies, pemphigus), or even normal anatomy (skin-fold infections on the face and nose) can all predispose the skin to infections. Every dog and cat has a resident population of bacteria that naturally resides on the skin, usually without causing any problems whatsoever. However, when the normal health and integrity of the skin are disrupted, disease-causing bacteria can multiply and overgrow the resident bacteria. When this happens, infections can gain a foothold.

In addition to a number of causes, bacterial skin infections can assume a number of appearances as well. *Pyoderma* is the term used to describe those skin infections that have pus (dead blood cells and tissue debris) as one of their features. Other infections may not have any pus, but instead may be characterized by many small scabs and crusts. Still others may appear as hair loss only, with little evidence of skin involvement. Recognizing which type of bacterial infection is involved is crucial, since treatment regimens can vary widely depending on the type.

Ringworm affecting the nose of a cat.

As the data presented in the table on page 32 testify, there are many medicated shampoos from which to choose to treat skin infections. Some require a prescription; others do not. If you plan to use a nonprescription shampoo, be certain to select the right one. Shampoos containing chlorhexidine, triclosan, or iodine are effective at fighting infections, but because most cats are sensitive to iodine, preparations containing iodine should not be used on them. Benzoyl peroxide is also a very effective ingredient against skin infections, yet few shampoos containing this chemical are available without a prescription from your veterinarian. Proper selection is vital, so ask your veterinarian for advice.

Major infections, such as those extending beneath the outer surface of the skin, and superficial infections that involve extensive areas of the skin surface should never be treated by pet owners. These need to be evaluated and treated by your veterinarian as soon as possible. This is true also for those seemingly minor infections that fail to resolve within a day or two. Specially formulated medicated shampoos; antibiotic, antifungal, and/or anti-inflammatory medications; or injections are required to treat these infections and prevent any undesirable after effects. Some cases may require surgical intervention before the healing process can be effected.

Hot Spots

A "hot spot," or acute moist dermatitis, is nothing more than a swollen, moist, raw area of infection that occurs on the surface of the skin. Traditionally, this term has been restricted to dogs, yet theoretically, cats can develop them also. The telltale signs associated with these moist lesions are an intense itching sensation, and rapid spread of the moist infection over the skin surface. You must be alert for signs of spreading. What starts out as a quarter-sized hot spot below the ear of a dog can spread over the entire neck and forequarters in only a matter of hours! In addition, unless you can prevent your pet from licking or scratching, this too will aggravate the condition further by keeping the infection moist and irritating the skin.

What causes hot spots? Most of the time, fleas or allergies are to blame, but anything that irritates the skin can be suspect. For instance, ear mites and ear infections can play a leading role in the development of hot spots around the head and ears. Usually the irritation caused by these dermatopathies or parasites induce the pet to chew, lick, or scratch at the affected sites. Once the skin becomes injured by these actions and the traumatized areas accumulate moisture through oozing blood and serum and through licking, an infection follows. Once the infection becomes established, the irritation intensifies, and the licking, chewing, and scratching follow suit. A vicious cycle develops.

Dogs and cats with long coats or heavy undercoats develop hot spots more readily than others. In addition, pets that have been translocated from northern, cooler climates into hot southern climates are prime candidates. Breed predispositions can occur as well, with Labrador retrievers and golden retrievers leading the list.

Treatment for hot spots should first be directed at drying the affected areas, followed by treating the infection itself. Clipping the hair from the affected regions provides an excellent way to allow air to circulate and help with the drying process. Don't worry about how your pet will look after the clipping; the hair will grow back! One word of caution, however: Because these lesions are often extremely painful, tranquilization and professional restraint may be needed before clipping can be performed safely. A drying agent should be applied directly to the moist lesions. Avoid using alcohol for this purpose, because you are liable to get bitten! As an alternative, you can use your pet's ear-cleaning solution. These solutions are designed as drying agents and are effective weapons against moist infections. Other so called "hot spot" remedies, most of which contain a drying substance plus an antimicrobial agent such as sulfur, will also prove effective, and can be purchased at your local pet store or through your veterinarian. Corn starch has also been used to absorb moisture, but remember that this substance has no antiseptic value; when it becomes saturated with tissue fluid, it can actually aggravate the condition if left on too long. Regardless of what type of agent you choose, it should be applied four to six times daily to be effective—more often if your pet has the propensity to lick. In addition, after each application of drying solution, a triple antibiotic cream or ointment can be spread over the lesion to enhance healing. (A triple antibiotic preparation is one that is compounded of three different antibiotics in a spreadable medium.)

For hot spots that encompass a large area or are actively spreading, antibiotics and anti-inflammatory medications are a must. Don't waste time trying to treat these at home. The sooner you get medical attention, the sooner you'll resolve the problem.

Skin-Fold Pyoderma (Intertrigo)

Some dogs and cats are prone to moist skin infections simply because of their anatomy. Skin-fold infections are a good example of this. Redundant folds of skin lead to poor air circulation within these areas, creating a warm, dark, moist environment, ideal for bacterial growth. For example, breeds with deep skin folds around

their nose and eyes, such as Pugs and Persian cats, are highly susceptible to nasal-fold infections. Pyodermas involving lip folds often appear in cocker spaniels and similar breeds, and can significantly add to the "bad breath" that many owners of these pets complain about. Similarly, dogs that have curly tails, such as Boston terriers, may have this problem occurring in the skin folds surrounding the tail.

The objectives for treatment of skin-fold pyoderma are to clear up any infection present and to maintain a dry environment within the affected areas. The first objective can be met by cleaning the affected areas daily with medicated shampoos or gels containing 2.5% benzoyl peroxide, then applying a drying agent (see "Hot Spots," page 98) to the skin between the folds. Once the initial infection has been resolved, periodic application (three to four times weekly) of the drying agent will help prevent reoccurrence. In difficult or recurring cases, cosmetic surgery, aimed at the removal of the offending skin folds, can be helpful.

Folliculitis

Folliculitis is the term given to any bacterial infection involving the hair follicles. The hallmark signs of folliculitis include the presence of numerous scabs and crusts, and/or small pustules, some of which may have tiny hairs extending from their centers. Pets suffering from folliculitis may actually look as though they have a

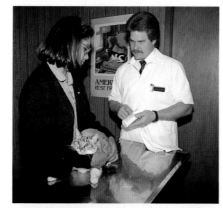

Consult your veterinarian before using any over-the-counter medication on your pet.

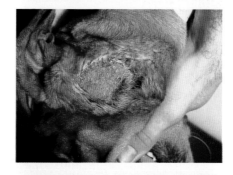

Acute moist dermatitis ("hot spot").

Lip-fold pyodermas are not uncommon in cocker spaniels.

bad case of hives. And, as you might expect, whenever the hair follicles are involved, hair loss usually follows soon after. As a result, the hair coats of dogs and cats afflicted with folliculitis often assume a "moth-eaten" appearance.

Oral antibiotics combined with medicated shampoos containing povidone iodine (dogs only), chlorhexidine, or 2.5% benzoyl peroxide are frequently used to treat folliculitis in dogs and cats. Daily application of medicated skin and coat sprays, containing similar ingredients, is also an effective part of any treatment program.

Impetigo

Impetigo, also known as "puppy pyoderma," typically affects puppies, usually less than six months of age. Characterized by the presence of numerous small pustules on the belly, inner legs, and armpits, impetigo is often incorrectly mistaken for ant or insect bites. Fortunately, this is one disease that pet owners needn't worry too much about. In most cases, applications of antibacterial shampoos will usually suffice. In some instances, the infection clears up spontaneously without any treatment at all. Recurrences of impetigo become rare as the puppy matures.

Juvenile Pyoderma

As with impetigo, juvenile pyoderma—"puppy strangles"—occurs primarily in puppies less than six months of age. But unlike the former disease, this dermatopathy can be a serious disease if left untreated. This type of infection localizes around the lips, eyelids, and ears of affected puppies, and often causes generalized facial swelling. In addition, enlargement of the lymph nodes in the neck usually accompanies episodes of juvenile pyoderma. Unless prompt therapy, consisting of antibiotics and steroids, is obtained, unsightly, irreversible scarring can be an unfortunate result of this disease.

Abscesses and Cellulitis

Both of these terms refer to bacterial infections that involve the deeper layers of the skin or underlying tissues. The difference between the two lies in the fact that true abscesses have distinct, defined boundaries, whereas cellulitis claims no boundaries. Pain and swelling are distinct features of both, and pus-draining tracts are often seen with the former. These dermatopathies are the most common cause of fever, depression, and loss of appetite in cats. Normally resulting from bite wounds acquired during fighting, feline abscesses arise most often on the face, on the back near the base of the tail, and on the legs. In fact, abscesses should be suspected whenever a cat is noticed limping.

Abscesses and cellulitis in dogs and cats warrant prompt veterinary attention. Since they involve the deeper layers of the skin, septicemia (blood poisoning) could result if neglected. If this happens, the infection could then spread to the internal

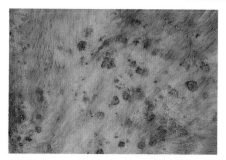

Folliculitis characterized by numerous scabs and crusts.

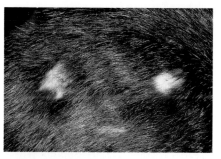

Impetigo.

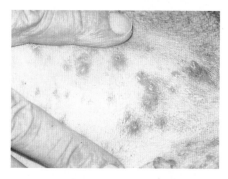

Bite wounds indicating the site of an abscess.

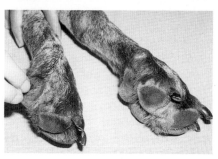

Interdigital pyoderma.

organs, including the heart and kidneys. To prevent this, treatment should include high dosages of antibiotics and, if indicated, surgical drainage of the abscess.

Pododermatitis (Interdigital Pyoderma)

Dermatopathies involving the feet of dogs and cats can be frustrating to deal with, since they can result from a number of sources. For example, allergies, parasites (mange, ringworm), foreign bodies (for example, grass burrs), and trauma (both physical and chemical) have all been implicated at one time or another. Dogs and cats kept in wet, unsanitary environments also are prone to develop this affliction. One possible way to separate the causes is to determine how many feet are involved. If just one foot is involved, trauma, parasites, or foreign bodies could be to blame. On the other hand, if multiple feet are affected, the source could be allergies or filthy environmental conditions. In most cases of pododermatitis, incessant licking and moist bacterial infections accompany the lesions.

After addressing the source of the pododermatitis, the infection should be treated by soaking the affected feet for 15 minutes, three to four times daily, in solutions containing povidone iodine (dogs only), chlorhexidine, or epsom salts. After soaking, the feet and toes should be dried thoroughly using a blow dryer or by applying some type of drying agent, such as ear-cleansing solution.

Seborrhea

Seborrhea is a term used to describe a condition in which abnormal skin growth and turnover occurs, with or without abnormal sebaceous gland activity (see "The Skin" page 13). This results in skin that is either excessively flaky or excessively greasy, depending on which type of seborrhea is involved. Primary seborrheas (those without any underlying cause) usually restrict themselves to dogs, with the exception of "stud tail" in cats (see "Stud Tail," page 115). Those breeds predisposed to primary seborrhea include Doberman pinschers, Irish setters, cocker spaniels, and springer spaniels. Secondary seborrhea can appear in both dogs and cats alike in response to some external or internal disturbance. Some of these potential problems, which include hormone imbalances, allergies, nutritional deficiencies, skin parasites, and infections, are listed in the table on page 80.

One type of seborrhea, called *seborrhea sicca*, is considered the dry form of the disease. When this occurs, dandruff-like flakes of skin result primarily because of abnormal skin cell turnover. Doberman pinschers are especially predisposed to this type of flaking, which can appear in great abundance all over the coat—much to the dismay of their owners. Itching may or may not be a factor in these cases. In contrast to seborrhea sicca, *seborrhea oleosa* is characterized by excess sebum production by the sebaceous glands. This makes the skin and coat excessively greasy and oily, and oftentimes leaves it inflamed and reeking with a bad odor. Secondary skin infections and itching are common with seborrhea oleosa.

In cases of secondary seborrhea (be it of either type), diagnosis and treatment of the underlying cause afford the most successful method of managing the dermatopathy. Other treatment methods useful for both primary and secondary seborrhea include daily dietary supplementation with balanced vitamin, mineral, and fatty acid preparations; weekly antiseborrheic shampoos; and, in the case of seborrhea sicca, daily application of moisturizing and emollient rinses or sprays. Brushing the coat at least twice a day is beneficial therapy as well.

Skin Calluses

Found primarily on the elbows, lower hind legs, and other pressure points that contact hard surfaces, calluses are certainly unsightly, yet normally pose no health threat. Sometimes, however, they can become infected and may need to be medicated. Because calluses are caused by lying on hard surfaces, this is the first item that needs correcting. If your porch or patio is concrete, provide carpeting, blankets, or towels on which your dog can lie. Soft bedding within dog houses will also ease the irritation placed on these pressure points. The calluses can be treated with skin moisturizers, petroleum jelly, and/or lanolin applied three to four times daily. These agents will help soften the calluses and stimulate new hair growth. Daily application of creams containing vitamin E have proven to be helpful in selected cases as well.

Neurodermatitis

Behavior is the responsible party for the formation of these dermatopathies, and this condition can affect both dogs and cats. In dogs, the common name for neurodermatitis is *acral lick dermatitis*. In cats, it is better known as *psychogenic hair loss*.

Acral lick dermatitis is identified by constant licking or chewing at an isolated region of the skin, usually somewhere on the legs. Quite often the area in question becomes thickened, raw, and ulcerated, with secondary infections by bacteria common. Boredom is thought to play a leading role in this disease; for lack of a better explanation, the dog has "nothing better to do"! In some instances, local inflammation of nerve endings, resulting from previous injuries or trauma to the site(s), or hypothyroidism (see "Thyroid Hormones," page 106) may be contributing factors.

Treatment of acral lick dermatitis consists of local application of medicated creams and ointments to help soothe the inflammation and prevent infection. Injections of anti-inflammatory drugs directly into the lesions may also be helpful. If boredom or some

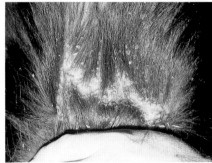

Seborrhea sicca.

Seborrhea oleosa. Note the yellow, greasy appearance of the skin.

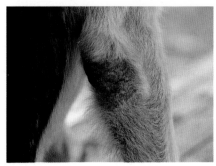

Elbow hygroma.

other underlying factor is involved, that needs to be addressed as well.

Neurodermatitis in cats classically presents itself as hair loss or broken hairs on the belly and inner thighs, or as a "stripe" of hair loss down the middle of the back. Infection may or may not be present. More than 90 percent of the time, the "emotional breeds"— the Siamese, Burmese, Abyssinian, and Himalayan—are involved. It appears that these are the breeds most likely to use licking and grooming as their means of releasing stress. And as every cat owner knows, a cat's tongue is more effective at removing hair than is the most efficient slicker brush that money can buy!

Emotional upset, caused by such things as changes in household routines, addition of a new pet into the house, or just simply being left alone, is usually the triggering factor for this dermatopathy. And since feline psychiatrists are few and far between, this is a difficult disease to treat. Eliminating the cause of the emotional stress is certainly the first place to start. Try to identify any changes that may have taken place in your or your cat's daily routine and, if possible, get them back to the way they were. If you have recently brought a new puppy or kitten into the household, are you inadvertently ignoring your older friend? If so, try showing this pet some extra attention. It may solve the problem. Likewise, if your cat gets upset when you leave, try leaving the television or radio on while you are gone. It is little details such as these that you need to focus on in order to reduce the stress that is underlying this problem.

In addition to the measures mentioned above, hormonal therapy has also been used with varying degrees of success to combat this disorder. Given either by pill or injection, these hormones, called progestins, exert a calming effect on the cat's behavior, making it less likely to lick indiscriminately. Finally, daily brushing is a must for these patients, not only to remove any dead hair present and stimulate regrowth, but to give your pet the added attention that could make the difference.

Hormonal Dermatopathies

As you may already know, hormones are compounds that control and modify specific functions within the body. Because their presence is so vital, it is easy to see how too much or too little of a specific hormone could upset the delicate balance within the body and lead to illness.

Since a healthy skin and coat are always in an active, dynamic state of growth and regeneration, abnormal changes in the blood levels of certain hormones cannot help but manifest themselves outwardly as dermatopathies. These hormones include thyroid hormones, steroid hormones, sex hormones, and insulin. When one or more of these hormones is present in abnormal amounts, the integument may show signs of symmetrical hair loss and increased pigmentation

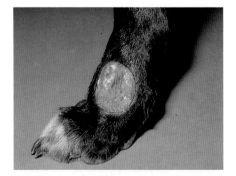

A severe case of acral lick dermatitis.

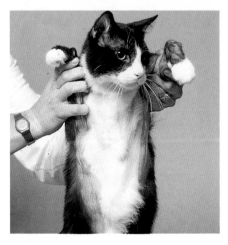

Hair loss on the abdomen of this feline due to nervous licking.

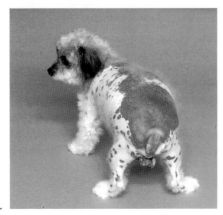

The results of hypothyroidism.

(darkening) of the skin. Itching is rarely a feature. While these outward changes may be the first signs of a problem detected by a pet owner, closer scrutinization will often reveal other signs of illness—signs having nothing to do with the skin and coat.

Thyroid Hormone

Since thyroid hormone is responsible for regulating overall body and skin metabolism, *hypothyroidism* (low levels of thyroid hormone) has a profound effect on the skin and coat. This disorder is usually seen only in dogs, with breeds such as Doberman pinschers, dachshunds, golden retrievers, and cocker spaniels affected the most. Canines suffering from this disorder tend to have thinned hair coats, including loss of the soft undercoats. The skin appears thicker than normal, and may have increased pigmentation. Seborrhea may occur, which could lead to itching. Affected dogs will tire easily, and may accumulate excess weight. Ear infections are often seen with hypothyroidism.

The causes of hypothyroidism are complicated and beyond the scope of this discussion, yet the diagnosis and treatment are not. Veterinarians have the ability to perform preliminary in-house blood tests to determine thyroid levels in pets suspected of having this disorder. If found positive for hypothyroidism, follow-up tests may be performed on the patient to confirm the diagnosis and to determine the actual extent of the problem. Treatment of hypothyroidism is not difficult: daily oral supplementation of thyroid hormone. In most cases, the medication must be given for the rest of the pet's life to prevent recurrences.

If hypothyroidism seems to limit itself to dogs; naturally occurring *hyperthyroidism* (high levels of thyroid hormone) does the same for cats. Too much of this hormone results in weight loss, a voracious appetite, and unkempt, greasy coats, among other signs. Cancer of the thyroid gland usually underlies hyperthyroidism, and treatment, which involves surgery or the use of anticancer drugs, is often unrewarding. In rare instances, over-supplementing thyroid hormone to hypothyroid dogs has resulted in signs of hyperthyroidism; reducing the levels administered resolves the problem swiftly.

Steroid Hormones

Even though they have received unfavorable publicity in recent years, steroid hormones serve more than 40 different functions within the body—all of vital importance. There are many types of steroid hormones produced by the body. In regard to the skin and coat, we are not concerned with the body-building types (anabolic steroids), but with a special group called *glucocorticosteroids*. Some familiar names within this classification include cortisone, prednisone, and prednisolone. Among their many functions, the one that stands out in both veterinary and human medicine is their ability to reduce inflammation. Dogs and cats are given these steroids to stop itching, relieve pain, prevent shock, and reduce inflammation caused by a wide variety of injuries or illnesses. Used appropriately, they are effective weapons that induce much needed relief to pets suffering from dermatopathies.

If steroids are so helpful, then why can't they be used all the time? The answer is this: Glucocorticosteroids, when given steadily over a long period of time, can have some very undesirable, even life-threatening side effects. Providing the body with a continuous supply of oral, injectable, or topical (creams and ointments) steroids may impair the animal's own ability to produce these compounds naturally, which could have fatal consequences. Furthermore, inappropriately high levels of steroid hormones within the body can suppress the body's immune system, leaving the dog or cat prone to other diseases, including cancer. As a result, whenever steroids are used in your pet, they should be administered only under the direct supervision of your veterinarian.

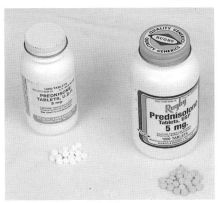

Steroids given over long periods of time can have undesirable, even life-threatening side effects.

High levels of glucocorticosteroids within the body can also be caused by a disease that affects the adrenal glands, the organs that normally produce steroids within the body. This condition is commonly known as Cushing's disease, and is more common in dogs than it is in cats. Pets with Cushing's disease display observable changes in the skin and coat, as well as in the other body systems. These changes can include thinning of the skin, seborrhea, increased pigmentation, and secondary bacterial infections. The hair is usually dry and brittle, and thin on both sides of the body. Signs unrelated to the skin often include a loss of muscle mass (resulting in a "pot-bellied" appearance), increased urination, and excessive panting.

Blood tests are required to confirm cases of Cushing's disease in pets. Besides overdosage of steroids, cancer is the primary cause of this disease. As a result, therapy includes either surgery or chemotherapy to reduce the secretion of hormones.

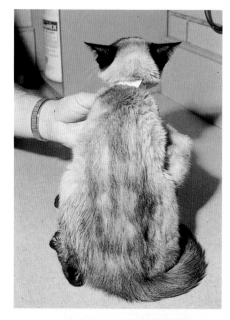

*Feline
endocrine
alopecia.*

*A severe case
of feline acne.*

Sex Hormones

Disruptions in the normal levels of sex hormones (estrogen and progesterone in females, testosterone in males) in dogs can also cause dermatopathies, most of which are manifested as symmetrical hair loss all over the body. In addition to this hair loss, increased skin pigmentation and seborrhea are seen in many cases. Diagnosis of this type of dermatopathy is based upon the history of the problem, upon the clinical signs seen, and upon ruling out other likely causes. Once diagnosed, treatment of the imbalance usually involves neutering (removal of the internal sex organs) or hormonal supplementation.

Cats can also be afflicted with similar hormone imbalances. When this occurs, it is given the proper name of *feline endocrine alopecia*. As mentioned previously, feline endocrine alopecia appears as a symmetrical loss of hair affecting the hind end, back thighs, and belly of neutered male and, in some instances, female cats. During the period of hair loss, the underlying skin usually shows no evidence of trauma or infection and doesn't appear to be itchy. It is important to point out that many veterinarians and researchers still dispute that this disease exists at all; many believe that some other dermatopathy is to blame for the symptoms. While this may be true, there is no denying that unexplained cases of progressive hair loss have been well documented in cats, especially neutered males. In absence of a better explanation, feline endocrine alopecia seems the likely suspect in these instances. Many of these cats respond positively to treatment consisting of special hormonal therapy given either in pill form or by injection. As a result, until further evidence to the contrary surfaces, feline endocrine alopecia will remain on the list of causes of unexplained hair loss in cats.

Insulin

The hallmark of the disease known as diabetes mellitus is an insufficient amount of insulin hormone, which lowers the body's ability to utilize carbohydrates. This, in turn, causes high levels of carbohydrate sugars to be present in the blood and urine. It also causes the body to draw on other sources of energy, such as protein and fat, to supply its needs. As we have seen, the skin and coat contain these compounds. As they are systematically removed, symmetrical hair loss, seborrhea, and secondary bacterial infections can result. Other nonrelated signs of diabetes include weight loss, increased urination, and cataracts. Obviously, identifying and treating the diabetes affords relief from its related dermatopathies and other complications.

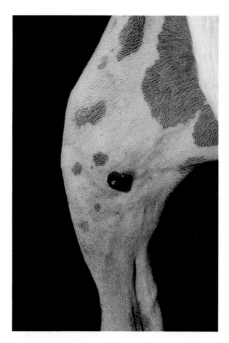

A biopsy is required to tell whether a tumor is benign or malignant.

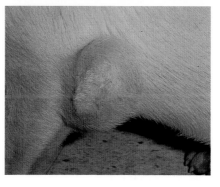

Lipoma

Acne

This skin condition is characterized by bumps, pustules, and/or blackheads on the chin of affected dogs and cats. And they don't even have to be teenagers to get it! The cause of acne has yet to be determined, but some feel that inadequate self-grooming in this area may be a big factor. Regardless, problems such as mange, ringworm, etc., must be ruled out before settling with a diagnosis of acne. Treatment for acne includes a thorough daily scrubbing with a mild, antibacterial soap or 2.5% benzoyl peroxide shampoo, followed by application of a drying agent (such as ear cleanser). This should eliminate the problem. In really difficult cases, antibiotics may be required to effect a complete cure.

Lumps or Masses on or Beneath the Skin

Any lump or bump found on or beneath the skin of your pet should warrant immediate attention. Oftentimes, the first thought that comes to mind is cancer or tumor, but other things can cause these as well. If felt beneath the skin, the lump could indeed be a tumor, but it could also be a cyst, abscess, or an area of chronic inflammation called a *granuloma*. If the mass is actually protruding from the skin, things to consider include granulomas and tumors (including warts). Do not rely on your interpretive abilities. Have the mass examined immediately by your veterinarian because, if it is something serious, early detection means greater chances for a complete recovery.

Tumors, or growths, involving the skin and underlying tissues can be either malignant or benign. The only way to differentiate which type they may be is by examining a biopsy specimen of the tumor under a microscope. The reason for this is that to the naked eye, these tumors can take on a wide variety of shapes and forms, from obvious, firm masses on or beneath the skin to raised, ulcerated lesions that may be easily mistaken for a hot spot or some similar nontumorous dermatopathy. There are many different types of tumors that affect dogs and cats. If you detect an abnormal mass, an abnormal pigment change, or any lesion slow to heal that involves your pet's skin, it could be cancer. Take your pet to the veterinarian for an examination promptly.

Tumors are a type of benign cancer that are very common in dogs, and deserve special mention. These lumps develop from the fatty tissue located just beneath the skin, and can reach quite considerable sizes. Older, overweight animals are more likely to develop these than others. Often these masses can be diagnosed in your veterinarian's office by using a needle to withdraw some of the fatty tissue for microscopic examination. Rarely do lipomas turn malignant; however, if not removed, each one should be rechecked periodically to confirm its benign status. Lipomas are generally uncommon in cats.

Cysts are nothing more than round sacs filled with fluid or debris. Sebaceous cysts are probably the most common type of cyst seen involving pets, and they mainly affect dogs. These firm, nodular structures can be found anywhere on the body that sebaceous glands are found (see "The Skin," page 13). Definitive treatment should include surgical removal or cauterization (burning) of the offending cyst.

Granulomas, unlike cysts, are solid structures composed mainly of fibrous tissue and inflammatory cells. Though this term is sometimes erroneously linked to certain disease conditions, such as the eosinophilic granuloma complex in cats, granulomas should be more accurately described as structures that form in response to a foreign body, bacterial, or fungal infection of the skin and body. For instance, thorns or slivers that penetrate the skin may stimulate this type of reaction. What the body is actually trying to do in these instances is to form a protective covering around the unwelcome foreign body, thereby effectively isolating it. In turn, this protective coating can harden and become noticeable to the touch. Again, diagnosis is made by microscopic examination or surgical excision.

Granulomas have also been associated with vaccination reactions, forming little lumps at the sites where the injections were given. In most cases, no treatment is needed for these, and most will go away with time. However, for these and other granulomas that are particularly persistent, surgical removal may be necessary.

Warts (papillomas) are familiar to almost everyone. Any breed of dog or cat can be affected by these cauliflower-like growths. Warts can show up on the eyelids, in the mouth, and anywhere on the body, including the feet. Some originate from the sebaceous glands of the skin; others develop from the epidermis itself. Regardless of their origin, they are usually benign in nature, and pose no threat to health. Some warts can get so large as to become traumatized and ulcerated, predisposing them to infection. In these cases, surgical removal under a local anesthetic provides the easiest and quickest method of treatment. And just in case you are thinking of doing so, *do not use human wart preparations on these warts*. If you do, you may harm your pet!

Pigment and Color Changes Involving the Skin and Hair

Melanin is the name of the pigment contained within the skin that helps determine skin and coat color in dogs and cats. Additionally, it helps protect the skin from the harmful effects of the sun's radiation. Solar dermatitis (see page 113) is a prime example of what insufficient levels of pigment can lead to. Skin cancer can be another unfortunate side effect of poorly pigmented skin exposed to the sun's ultraviolet rays.

Genetics plays an important role in the amount of pigmentation within the skin and hair. *Albino* dogs and cats are totally devoid of pigment whatsoever. You can imagine how sensitive they are to normal, or even reduced levels of sunlight. Less dramatic genetic disorders involving melanin can exist as well. Interestingly enough, many of these are associated with deafness in the affected animal. White-haired, blue-eyed cats are a good example of this phenomenon.

Hypopigmentation, or underpigmentation, can result from other factors besides genetics. Skin that has been burned or, conversely, has been frostbitten, will often retain a much lighter color than the surrounding skin. Scars obtained from wounds or surgery may also share this characteristic. Certain inflammatory skin diseases, such as pemphigus, may cause hypopigmentation of the affected skin, especially around the lips and nose.

Like its counterpart, hyperpigmentation, also known as overpigmentation or *acanthosis nigricans*, can have a genetic basis, but its sudden or gradual appearance over time could mean that some underlying disease is to blame. Probably the most common cause of skin or hair darkening is inflammation. Long-term exposure to allergies, parasites, and skin infections can gradually lead to these changes. Localized cases of hyperpigmentation have been known to appear following the injection of a drug or vaccine. The increase in skin temperature that accompanies some inflammatory processes can cause transient darkening of the coat, either locally or widespread over the body. Notice that the adjective *transient* was used; in most instances, the normal hair color will return at the next hair cycle.

Other causes of hyperpigmentation can include hormonally related derma-

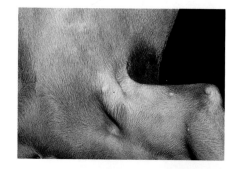

Sebaceous cysts.

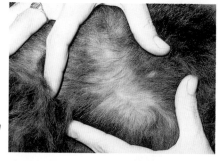

After shaving, this hair grew in a different color.

Hyper-pigmentation caused by long-term inflammation.

topathies, such as Cushing's disease and hypothyroidism, chronic irritation (licking or rubbing), and cancer. As far as the latter is concerned, *melanoma* (pigmented skin tumor) is one of the most serious types of cancer that can affect dogs and cats, since it can spread rapidly. Melanomas are usually blue-black or brown in color, and can assume a number of different shapes. Any unexplained areas of hyper-pigmentation involving the skin should be suspect, and checked out immediately.

Thinned hair coat on a blue Doberman.

Solar Dermatitis

Ultraviolet rays from the sun contacting lightly pigmented skin are responsible for this skin disorder, which is also known as photodermatitis and "collie nose." In fact, it can be equated to a severe case of sunburn! Reddened, ulcerated sores appearing on the nose and ears are common clinical signs associated with photodermatitis. In addition, chronic solar dermatitis can often lead to skin cancer. Dogs and cats with white coats are predisposed to this disease due to reduced amounts of protective pigmentation in their skin.

Existing sores should be treated with topical antibiotic creams to control infection. Exposure to the sun's rays needs to be reduced as well. Keeping your pet indoors on sunny days will reduce this exposure. Sunblocks or sunscreens with ratings of 15 or higher may be applied directly to the affected areas to effectively block

Nasal solar dermatitis.

out the ultraviolet rays. If used, they should be reapplied often to insure maximum effectiveness.

Hair Loss Not Related to Disease

There are a few instances in which lack or loss of hair is not caused by a disease, but by normal genetic or physiological factors. Genetic examples include Mexican hairless and certain Chihuahua dogs, "blue" Doberman pinschers and dachshunds, as well as the normal hair thinning seen on the heads of cats just in front of the ears (preauricular baldness).

One example of a physiological factor is *telogen effluvium*. This complex term refers to hair loss caused by stress. Pregnancy, illness, trauma, etc., can all cause enough stress on the body to cause this type of hair loss. A simple trip to the veterinary office can induce this as well. Did you ever wonder why your pet sheds so much whenever you take it to the veterinarian? Telogen effluvium, acting as a built-in defense mechanism, is to blame. With the loosening of the hair within the hair follicles that occurs, anything that tries to grab an unwilling pet is probably bound to end up with a mouthful (or, in our case, a handful) of hair instead. You might liken the reaction to that of the lizard that loses its tail when threatened.

Another example of a physiological factor is the phenomenon where the normal hair cycle suddenly stops or becomes dormant. Stress factors similar to those seen with telogen effluvium, such as illnesses or traumatic incidents, can cause the hair cycle to temporarily come to a halt, leaving no replacement for the dead hair that is eventually shed. Another instance where this phenomenon could occur is when hair is shorn off close to the skin using clippers. There have been cases in which hair that had been removed prior to performing a surgical procedure has taken months to grow back. Unfortunately, the reason for this still remains unknown, yet the good news is that the hair loss is not permanent; it will eventually grow back.

Dermatopathies Unique to Cats

Miliary Dermatitis

Have you ever found a bunch of tiny crusts or scabs around the neck or head of your cat? If so, you were observing the skin condition known as *feline miliary dermatitis*. You may have heard your veterinarian talk of this, but its significance is often misunderstood. Miliary dermatitis actually refers to the unique way a cat's skin reacts to certain irritants or diseases. It is not a disease entity in itself; it is simply a sign of disease. These crusty lesions, which can be found anywhere on the body, are the irritating source of constant licking, rubbing, and scratching. Fleas cause more than 75 percent of the cases of miliary dermatitis. Ringworm, allergies, mange, and fatty acid deficiencies are also among the other notable causes.

The first step in treating a cat with miliary dermatitis is to identify and treat the dermatopathy that is causing the problem. At the same time, anti-inflammatory drugs prescribed by your veterinarian can be used to help relieve the discomfort and extent of the miliary reaction.

Eosinophilic Granuloma Complex

As with feline miliary dermatitis, this disorder is often incorrectly given disease status. In actuality, it is merely an outward sign or side effect of another underlying dermatopathy, usually an allergy of some sort. Ulcerations on the lips, fire-red bumps or elevations on the belly or inner thighs, or raised, yellow-pink nodules on the back part of the hind legs are the most prevalent signs seen with this complex. If improperly diagnosed, the lesions could be easily mistaken for skin cancer. Treatment for eosinophilic granuloma complex is essentially the same as that for miliary dermatitis; however, improvement may not come as quickly. Recurrences can and do occur, especially in those instances in which the underlying disorder cannot be controlled.

Lip ulcers caused by ecsinophilic granuloma complex.

Stud Tail

"Stud tail" is a seborrhea-like skin condition commonly seen in male cats, although females can suffer from it as well. Characterized by a buildup of yellow-black, greasy deposits at the base of the tail, stud tail is caused by hyperactivity of sebaceous glands located in this particular region. Treatment consists of gentle cleansing of the affected area with a mild soap or shampoo, followed by the application of some type of drying agent, such as isopropyl alcohol or an ear-cleansing solution. As a general rule, treatment should be performed two to three times weekly to help keep this condition under control.

Chapter 8

First Aid for Grooming Injuries

If you happen to "quick" a toenail or get soap in your pet's eyes, don't panic! Below are some first aid techniques applicable to these and other situations that you might encounter when grooming your pet. If a serious injury occurs, contact your veterinarian immediately for instructions on any further first aid steps that need to be taken prior to the trip to the hospital.

Bleeding Nails

If you are properly following the home grooming program, this event will invariably happen at one time or another. So don't feel bad, your pet will recover! Just stay calm and follow the following procedures:

1. With a clean cloth, tissue, or gauze pad apply direct pressure to the bleeding end of the nail for five to ten minutes. If you wish, you can even tape a piece of tissue or gauze to the end of the nail.

2. If available, apply clotting powder to the end of the affected nail using a cotton-tipped applicator or your finger. Reapply as needed.

Cuts

The three most common causes of cuts and lacerations when grooming are: (1) the improper use and care of clipper blades; (2) careless attempts to remove mats and tangles with scissors; and (3) a pet that does not want to be groomed. If such an injury does occur, follow these guidelines:

- If the wound is bleeding profusely, apply direct pressure for a minimum of five minutes, using a gauze pad or clean cloth. Do not try to wash the wound, because this will just aggravate the bleeding. Seek veterinary assistance at once.

An allergic reaction to a medicated shampoo.

- If there is little or no bleeding from the cut or laceration, use a mild hand soap or hydrogen peroxide to clean the wound. Rinse thoroughly and blot dry, preferably using a sterile gauze pad.
- Apply an antibiotic ointment or cream to the wound three times daily for five to seven days to help prevent infection. Light bandaging is optional, but it may prevent licking or chewing by your pet.
- If at any time signs of infection appear (redness, swelling, heat, and pain), contact your veterinarian.

Clipper Burns

Clipper burns is a catchall phrase used to describe any injury or irritation caused by the use of electric clippers. Clipper burn can be caused by: (1) the actual blades becoming too hot during the clipping procedure and burning the skin; (2) Broken teeth on the clipper blade scraping or raking the skin surface, causing abrasions; or (3) dull blades pulling the hairs from their follicles, creating localized inflammation.

Obviously the best way to treat clipper burn is to prevent it in the first place by properly caring for clipper blades. However, if it does happen:

- Scrub the region with soap and water, then dry well.
- After drying, apply an antibiotic ointment or cream to the wound three times daily for five to seven days to help prevent infection.
- If the burn seems to be especially bothersome to the pet, over-the-counter preparations containing aloe or topical anesthetics can provide soothing relief when applied three times daily.

Allergic Reactions

Allergic reactions that occur after application of a noninsecticidal topical spray or shampoo are normally characterized by intense itching and reddening of the skin. They are rarely life threatening. If an insecticide is involved, however, this is not always the case. Signs associated with this type of poisoning can include vomiting, diarrhea, excessive salivation, and pinpoint pupil size. The presence of any of these signs warrants immediate action. Since cats and young dogs are the most sensitive to insecticides, most cases of allergic reactions and poisonings from these products can be prevented by *making sure* that the product you are using is safe for cats or for young puppies and kittens.

In the case of an allergic reaction, follow these procedures:

- Rinse your pet thoroughly with water to remove the offending agent. Cold water is an effective anti-itch remedy, and should be used if itching is a component of the reaction.
- If the above action fails to provide relief, or if swelling or any other abnormal signs appear, contact your veterinarian immediately. An antihistamine or anti-inflammatory injection may be needed.

In the case of an insecticidal poisoning, follow these procedures:

- Rinse your pet off thoroughly with cool water.
- Seek veterinary help immediately. In most cases, an antidote is available to counteract the harmful effects of the poison. Be certain to take the bottle containing the dip or shampoo used with you to the veterinary clinic.

Cracked Pads

Although cracked foot pads are rarely a grooming injury, first aid for this problem in dogs and cats is worth mentioning. Cracked pads can result from contact with hard surfaces, foreign objects such as rocks or glass, and even nutritional deficiencies. Since the pads are composed of a very thick layer of dead epithelial cells, these cracks or fissures normally pose no great problems in themselves. However, there have been cases in which they have enlarged and continued to penetrate deeper into the pad tissue, leading to tenderness and lameness. They could also potentially act as a trap for foreign matter, which could lead to further trauma and infection. As a result, if you notice such a crack, manage it in the following fashion:

- For very minor, uncontaminated superficial fissures, a small amount of instant glue or adhesive applied into the crack may be used. Be certain to keep your pet from licking the area until completely dry.
- For deeper cracks, wash the area with soap and water. Be sure to rinse and dry well. Then seal the crack with cyanoacrylate glue. *Note*: For those cracks that appear infected, or are causing obvious signs of lameness, do not apply glue. Instead, veterinary attention should be obtained.

Shampoo in the Eyes

If for some reason you happen to get soap or shampoo in your pet's eyes during a bath, immediate action should help prevent injury to the cornea. This includes:

- Flushing the affected eye with copious amounts of clean water. *Do not* apply any more ointment or mineral oil to the eye, since this could seal in the offending agent.
- If the eye appears reddened, or if your pet appears to be squinting, contact your veterinarian. Try to prevent your pet from rubbing or pawing at the affected eye until you reach the clinic.

Acknowledgments

The author wishes to thank the following individuals for their contributions:

David Chester, DVM, MS for his professional expertise and input; Claudia Chancellor and Albert Cisneros for their cosmetic grooming guidelines; Fredric L. Frye, DVM, MS and Kerry V. Kern for reading the manuscript and making many valuable suggestions; Sandra G. Pinson, Jill Mathis, and Dennis Dunleavy for their artistic contributions; and my wife Tracy, for her patience.

The author would also like to acknowledge those published sources used to verify and support much of the information contained herein:

Muller, Kirk, and Scott, *Small Animal Dermatology*, 4th Ed., W.B. Saunders Co., 1989.

Current Veterinary Therapy X, Edited by Robert W. Kirk, DVM, W.B. Saunders Co., 1989.

Current Veterinary Therapy IX, Edited by Robert W. Kirk, DVM, W.B. Saunders Co., 1986.

Nutrition and Management of Dogs and Cats, Ralston Purina Company, 1981.

Photo Credits

American Kennel Club: 124,125. Biomedical Learning Resource Center, College of Veterinary Medicine, Texas A&M University: 15; 18; 36; 37; 40; 82, left; 83, top, center; 87, bottom; 90; 91, top, bottom; 94–97; 100, center, bottom; 101; 104, top, center; 105; 106; 108; 109; 112; 113, top; 115; 117. Eugene Butenas (LCA): 4, bottom; 8; 124. Jane Donahue (Moments by Jane, Wellesley, MA): inside front cover–1; 4, top; 62; 116, bottom; 128–inside back cover. Dennis Dunleavy: 9; 12, top; 23, top, bottom left; 28; 30; 31, top; 33; 38, top; 42; 43; 45, bottom; 46–52; 53, top; 58; 59; 83, bottom; 86, top, center; 107. Jill Mathis: 8; 12, bottom; 13; 16; 19; 22; 23, bottom right; 26; 27; 29; 31, bottom; 38, bottom; 41; 44; 45, top; 53, bottom; 54; 55; 82, top right; 86, bottom; 87, top, center; 91, center; 100, top; 104, bottom; 113, bottom. Larry Naples (LCA): 116, top left. Aaron Norman: 5; 61; 116, top right; 120; 121.

Index

About the Author

Chris C. Pinney, DVM, is a practicing veterinary clinician and surgeon in San Antonio, Texas, and an avid pet owner as well. He has written numerous articles on veterinary medicine and pet ownership for scientific journals and lay magazines alike. Dr. Pinney is also host of his own television segment which spotlights pets and pet health care.

Useful Literature and Addresses

Books

Behrend, Katrin.
Cats: A Complete Pet Owner's Manual.
Barron's, New York, 1990.

Fenger, Diane and Steinle, Arlene F.
The Standard Book of Dog Grooming.
Denlingers, Fairfax, Virginia, 1983.

Gold, Charlotte.
Grooming Dogs for Profit.
Howell, New York, 1986.

Klever, Ulrich.
The Complete Book of Dog Care.
Barron's, New York, 1989.

Organizations

International Professional
Groomers, Inc.
P.O. Box 336
Concordia, Kansas 66901

National Dog Groomers Association
of America
P.O. Box 101
Clark, Pennsylvania 16113

Professional Pet Groomers
Certification Program
24622 Ford Road
Dearborn, Michigan 48127